ABA CURRICULUM FOR THE COMMON CORE

Programs and Materials for Teaching ELA and Math
in Special Education Using Applied Behavior Analysis

By Sam Blanco, MSEd, BCBA
for Different Roads to Learning

Different Roads
Tools for kids on the spectrum since 1995.

*ABA Curriculum for the Common Core: Kindergarten
Programs and Materials for Teaching ELA and Math
in Special Education Using Applied Behavior Analysis*

Copyright © 2014 Different Roads to Learning, Inc.

Published by
Different Roads to Learning, Inc.
37 East 18th Street, 10th Floor
New York, NY 10003
tel: 212.604.9637 | fax: 212.206.9329
www.difflearn.com

Printed in the United States

Library of Congress Number: 2014951907
ISBN Number: 978-09907083-0-8

Table of Contents

Foreword

We're thrilled to introduce this pioneering curriculum to teach each Common Core standard in special education settings. The Common Core is vague at best when it comes to its application to students with special needs, autism, and developmental disabilities. This curriculum aims to bridge the gap by equipping teachers with a companion curriculum that specifically addresses the learning needs of students in Special Education using the evidence-based principles of Applied Behavior Analysis. The kit provides both the materials and programs to teach each Kindergarten standard in English Language Arts and Math.

Our kit details each Common Core standard along with the Teaching Procedure, Discriminative Stimulus (Sd), and Materials required for teaching. The critical component of each program is the list of targets that drill down into the standard. It breaks each Common Core standard down into prerequisite skills that students need to master in order to meet the standard. Each task is presented within a data sheet so that the instructor may notate when the target was introduced, when it was mastered, and if it has been generalized for each student. Comprehensive Data Sheets for accurate record keeping are included, along with samples of how to complete them. In addition, a thorough how-to guide presents the main tenets of Applied Behavior Analysis (ABA), giving staff an accessible understanding of Motivation and Reinforcement, Pairing, Prompting, Generalization, Natural Environment Teaching, and Data Collection.

The key emphasis is on providing meaningful access to the standards by ensuring that we are teaching at a student's current skill level. By drilling down into each standard and breaking it into teachable steps and relying on the data collected for each student, we ensure that we are teaching at the edge of our students' abilities. Furthermore, by breaking each standard down and drilling into the prerequisite skills, the opportunity exists to use these Kindergarten programs for older students who are not developmentally able to meet grade-level standards.

The materials included in the kit have been carefully selected to not only assess and teach each standard and prerequisite skill, but to be wonderful additions to any classroom setting. The materials are versatile and can be used during more intensive teaching and one-to-one, as well as during center time and for independent play.

The goal of this curriculum kit is to make the Common Core accessible and relevant to students with autism and special needs. By equipping teachers with teachable steps for each and every standard and pairing the teaching with motivating, versatile materials, the *ABA Curriculum for the Common Core* puts Kindergarten students in Special Education on the path to achieving success.

— Different Roads to Learning

English Language Arts

In the table below, you will find each Common Core State Standard (CCSS) listed by Strand, Cluster, and Code, along with the correlating Kit Materials. This grid serves as a quick reference of the CCSS and the items from the *ABA Curriculum for the Common Core Kit* that you'll need for teaching.

STRAND & CLUSTER	CCSS CODE	STANDARD	TEACHING MATERIALS*
STRAND: READING/LITERATURE			
Key Ideas and Details	RL.K.1	With prompting and support, ask and answer questions about key details in a text.	• *Reading Comprehension Cubes* • *Differentiated Instruction Cubes* • *What Happened? ConversaCards* • Storybook from the classroom
	RL.K.2	With prompting and support, retell familiar stories, including key details.	• *Reading Comprehension Cubes* • *What Happened? ConversaCards* • *Differentiated Instruction Cubes* • Classroom reading materials
	RL.K.3	With prompting and support, identify characters, settings, and major events in a story.	• *Reading Comprehension Cubes* • *Differentiated Instruction Cubes* • Storybook from the classroom
Craft and Structure	RL.K.4	Ask and answer questions about unknown words in a text.	• *Differentiated Instruction Cubes* • *Following Auditory Directions* • Storybook or other reading materials from classroom
	RL.K.5	Recognize common types of texts (e.g., storybooks, poems).	• *Reading Comprehension Cubes* • Reading materials from classroom
	RL.K.6	With prompting and support, name the author and illustrator of a story and define the role of each in telling the story	• *Differentiated Instruction Cubes* • *Reading Comprehension Cubes* • Storybook or other reading materials from classroom
Integration of Knowledge and Ideas	RL.K.7	With prompting and support, describe the relationship between illustrations and the story in which they appear (e.g., what moment in a story an illustration depicts).	• *Differentiated Instruction Cubes* • Storybook or other reading materials from classroom
	RL.K.8	(RL.K.8 not applicable to literature)	N/A
	RL.K.9	With prompting and support, compare and contrast the adventures and experiences of characters in familiar stories.	• Storybook or other reading materials from classroom • Index cards, visual prompts
Range of Reading and Level of Text Complexity	RL.K.10	Actively engage in group reading activities with purpose and understanding.	• *Reading Comprehension Cubes* • *Differentiated Instruction Cubes* • *All Around Learning Circle Time Activity Set* • Storybook or other reading materials from classroom

*Teaching Materials listed in italics are included in the kit; those not italicized are not included and can be found in your classroom.

English Language Arts

STRAND & CLUSTER	CCSS CODE	STANDARD	TEACHING MATERIALS*
STRAND: READING/INFORMATIONAL TEXT			
Key Ideas and Details	RI.K.1	With prompting and support, ask and answer questions about key details in a text.	• *Reading Comprehension Cubes* • *Differentiated Instruction Cubes* • Informational text from the classroom
	RI.K.2	With prompting and support, identify the main topic and retell key details of a text.	• *Reading Comprehension Cubes* • *Differentiated Instruction Cubes* • *What Happened? ConversaCards* • Informational text from the classroom
	RI.K.3	With prompting and support, describe the connection between two individuals, events, ideas, or pieces of information in a text.	• *Differentiated Instruction Cubes* • Informational text from the classroom
Craft and Structure	RI.K.4	With prompting and support, ask and answer questions about unknown words in a text.	• *Reading Comprehension Cubes* • *Differentiated Instruction Cubes* • Informational text from the classroom
	RI.K.5	Identify the front cover, back cover, and title page of a book.	• *Differentiated Instruction Cubes* • Classroom reading materials
	RI.K.6	Name the author and illustrator of a text and define the role of each in presenting the ideas or information in a text.	• *Differentiated Instruction Cubes* • *Reading Comprehension Cubes* • Informational text from the classroom
Integration of Knowledge and Ideas	RI.K.7	With prompting and support, describe the relationship between illustrations and the text in which they appear (e.g., what person, place, thing, or idea in the text an illustration depicts).	• *Differentiated Instruction Cubes* • Informational text from the classroom
	RI.K.8	With prompting and support, identify the reasons an author gives to support points in a text.	• *Reading Comprehension Cubes* • *Differentiated Instruction Cubes* • Informational text from classroom
	RI.K.9	With prompting and support, identify basic similarities in and differences between two texts on the same topic (e.g., in illustrations, descriptions, or procedures).	• *Differentiated Instruction Cubes* • Two informational texts from the classroom on the same topic
Range of Reading and Level of Text Complexity	RI.K.10	Actively engage in group reading activities with purpose and understanding.	• *Reading Comprehension Cubes* • *Differentiated Instruction Cubes* • *All Around Learning Circle Time Activity Set* • Informational texts or other reading materials from classroom

*Teaching Materials listed in italics are included in the kit; those not italicized are not included and can be found in your classroom.

English Language Arts

STRAND & CLUSTER	CCSS CODE	STANDARD	TEACHING MATERIALS*
STRAND: READING/FOUNDATIONAL SKILLS			
Print Concepts	RF.K.1	Demonstrate understanding of the organization and basic features of print.	*See:* RF.K.1.a, RF.K.1.b, RF.K.1.c, RF.K.1.d
	RF.K.1.a	Follow words from left to right, top to bottom, and page by page.	• Classroom reading materials
	RF.K.1.b	Recognize that spoken words are represented in written language by specific sequences of letters.	• *Letters Pocket Chart Card Set* • *Sight Words Pocket Chart Card Set* • *Mid-Sized Pocket Chart* • *Chunk Stacker*
	RF.K.1.c	Understand that words are separated by spaces in print.	• *Writing and Art Kit* • Popsicle sticks (optional)
	RF.K.1.d	Recognize and name all upper- and lowercase letters of the alphabet.	• *Letters Pocket Chart Card Set* • *Differentiated Instruction Cubes* • *Mid-Sized Pocket Chart*
Phonological Awareness	RF.K.2	Demonstrate understanding of spoken words, syllables, and sounds (phonemes).	*See:* RF.K.2.a, RF.K.2.b, RF.K.2.c, RF.K.2.d, RF.K.2.e
	RF.K.2.a	Recognize and produce rhyming words.	• *Chunk Stacker* • *Differentiated Instruction Cubes* • *Letters Pocket Chart Card Set* • *Sight Words Pocket Chart Card Set* • *Mid-Sized Pocket Chart*
	RF.K.2.b	Count, pronounce, blend, and segment syllables in spoken words.	• *Sight Words Pocket Chart Card Set* • *Mid-Sized Pocket Chart* • Index Cards
	RF.K.2.c	Blend and segment onsets and rimes of single-syllable spoken words.	• *Letters Pocket Chart Card Set* • *Chunk Stacker*
	RF.K.2.d	Isolate and pronounce the initial, medial vowel, and final sounds (phonemes) in three-phoneme (consonant-vowel-consonant, or CVC) words.* (This does not include CVCs ending with /l/, /r/, or /x/.) *Words, syllables, or phonemes written in /slashes/ refer to their pronunciation or phonology. Thus, /CVC/ is a word with three phonemes regardless of the number of letters in the spelling of the word.	• *Letters Pocket Chart Card Set* • *Mid-Sized Pocket Chart* • *Chunk Stacker* • *Differentiated Instruction Cubes*
	RF.K.2.e	Add or substitute individual sounds (phonemes) in simple, one-syllable words to make new words.	• *Letters Pocket Chart Card Set* • *Mid-Sized Pocket Chart* • *Differentiated Instruction Cubes*

*Teaching Materials listed in italics are included in the kit; those not italicized are not included and can be found in your classroom.

STRAND & CLUSTER	CCSS CODE	STANDARD	TEACHING MATERIALS*
STRAND: READING/FOUNDATIONAL SKILLS *(continued)*			
Phonics and Word Recognition	RF.K.3	Know and apply grade-level phonics and word analysis skills in decoding words.	*See:* RF.K.3.a, RF.K.3.b, RF.K.3.c, RF.K.3.d
	RF.K.3.a	Demonstrate basic knowledge of one-to-one letter-sound correspondences by producing the primary sound or many of the most frequent sounds for each consonant.	• *Letters Pocket Chart Card Set* • *Differentiated Instruction Cubes* • *Mid-Sized Pocket Chart*
	RF.K.3.b	Associate the long and short sounds with the common spellings (graphemes) for the five major vowels.	• *Differentiated Instruction Cubes* • *Letters Pocket Chart Card Set* • *Mid-Sized Pocket Chart*
	RF.K.3.c	Read common high-frequency words by sight (e.g., the, of, to, you, she, my, is, are, do, does).	• *Sight Words Pocket Chart Card Set* • *Differentiated Instruction Cubes* • *Chunk Stacker*
	RF.K.3.d	Distinguish between similarly spelled words by identifying the sounds of the letters that differ.	• *Chunk Stacker* • *Letters Pocket Chart Card Set* • *Mid-Sized Pocket Chart* • Index Cards
Fluency	RF.K.4	Read emergent-reader texts with purpose and understanding.	• *Reading Comprehension Cubes* • *Differentiated Instruction Cubes* • Classroom reading materials
STRAND: WRITING			
Text Types and Purposes	W.K.1	Use a combination of drawing, dictating, and writing to compose opinion pieces in which they tell a reader the topic or the name of the book they are writing about and state an opinion or preference about the topic or book (e.g., My favorite book is...).	• *Writing and Art Kit* • Storybook from the classroom
	W.K.2	Use a combination of drawing, dictating, and writing to compose informative/explanatory texts in which they name what they are writing about and supply some information about the topic.	• *Writing & Art Kit*
	W.K.3	Use a combination of drawing, dictating, and writing to narrate a single event or several loosely linked events, tell about the events in the order in which they occurred, and provide a reaction to what happened.	• *Writing & Art Kit*
Production and Distribution of Writing	W.K.4	(W.K.4 begins in grade 3)	N/A
	W.K.5	With guidance and support from adults, respond to questions and suggestions from peers and add details to strengthen writing as needed.	• *Differentiated Instruction Cubes*
	W.K.6	With guidance and support from adults, explore a variety of digital tools to produce and publish writing, including in collaboration with peers.	• Computers, tablets, cameras

*Teaching Materials listed in italics are included in the kit; those not italicized are not included and can be found in your classroom.

STRAND & CLUSTER	CCSS CODE	STANDARD	TEACHING MATERIALS*
STRAND: WRITING *(continued)*			
Research to Build and Present Knowledge	W.K.7	Participate in shared research and writing projects (e.g., explore a number of books by a favorite author and express opinions about them).	• *Differentiated Instruction Cubes* • Storybooks by the same author or about the same topic
	W.K.8	With guidance and support from adults, recall information from experiences or gather information from provided sources to answer a question.	• Visual, textual or gestural prompts during conversation
	W.K.9	(W.K.9 begins in grade 4)	N/A
Range of Writing	W.K.10	(W.K.10 begins in grade 3)	N/A
STRAND: SPEAKING AND LISTENING			
Comprehension and Collaboration	SL.K.1	Participate in collaborative conversations with diverse partners about kindergarten topics and texts with peers and adults in small and larger groups.	*See:* SL.K.1.a, SL.K.1.b
	SL.K.1.a	Follow agreed-upon rules for discussions (e.g., listening to others and taking turns speaking about the topics and texts under discussion).	• *What Do You Like? ConversaCards* • *ConversaCards* (any set)
	SL.K.1.b	Continue a conversation through multiple exchanges.	• *ConversaCards* (any set)
	SL.K.2	Confirm understanding of a text read aloud or information presented orally or through other media by asking and answering questions about key details and requesting clarification if something is not understood.	• *Reading Comprehension Cubes* • *Differentiated Instruction Cubes* • Classroom reading materials
	SL.K.3	Ask and answer questions in order to seek help, get information, or clarify something that is not understood.	• *ConversaCards* (any set)
Presentation of Knowledge and Ideas	SL.K.4	Describe familiar people, places, things, and events and, with prompting and support, provide additional detail.	• Visual, textual or gestural prompts during conversation
	SL.K.5	Add drawings or other visual displays to descriptions as desired to provide additional detail.	• *Writing & Art Kit*
	SL.K.6	Speak audibly and express thoughts, feelings, and ideas clearly.	• *What Do You Like? ConversaCards* • *What Do You Need? ConversaCards*

*Teaching Materials listed in italics are included in the kit; those not italicized are not included and can be found in your classroom.

English Language Arts

STRAND & CLUSTER	CCSS CODE	STANDARD	TEACHING MATERIALS*
STRAND: LANGUAGE			
Conventions of Standard English	L.K.1	Demonstrate command of the conventions of standard English grammar and usage when writing or speaking.	*See:* L.K.1.a, L.K.1.b, L.K.1.c, L.K.1.d, L.K.1.e, L.K.1.f
	L.K.1.a	Print many upper- and lowercase letters.	• *Writing & Art Kit*
	L.K.1.b	Use frequently occurring nouns and verbs.	• *What Do You Do With It? ConversaCards*
	L.K.1.c	Form regular plural nouns orally by adding /s/ or /es/ (e.g., dog, dogs; wish, wishes).	• Boxes, a variety of classroom or household items
	L.K.1.d	Understand and use question words (interrogatives) (e.g., who, what, where, when, why, how).	• *What Happened? ConversaCards* • *What Do you Need? ConversaCards*
	L.K.1.e	Use the most frequently occurring prepositions (e.g., to, from, in, out, on, off, for, of, by, with).	• *I Can Do That! Game* • *Following Auditory Directions*
	L.K.1.f	Produce and expand complete sentences in shared language activities.	• Visual, textual or gestural prompts during conversation
	L.K.2	Demonstrate command of the conventions of standard English capitalization, punctuation, and spelling when writing.	*See:* L.K.2.a, L.K.2.b, L.K.2.c, L.K.2.d
	L.K.2.a	Capitalize the first word in a sentence and the pronoun "I".	• *Writing & Art Kit*
	L.K.2.b	Recognize and name end punctuation.	• *Differentiated Instruction Cubes*
	L.K.2.c	Write a letter or letters for most consonant and short-vowel sounds (phonemes).	• *Writing & Art Kit*
	L.K.2.d	Spell simple words phonetically, drawing on knowledge of sound-letter relationships.	• *Writing & Art Kit*
Knowledge of Language	L.K.3	(L.K.3 begins in grade 2)	N/A

*Teaching Materials listed in italics are included in the kit; those not italicized are not included and can be found in your classroom.

English Language Arts

STRAND & CLUSTER	CCSS CODE	STANDARD	TEACHING MATERIALS*
STRAND: LANGUAGE *(continued)*			
Vocabulary Acquisition and Use	L.K.4	Determine or clarify the meaning of unknown and multiple-meaning words and phrases based on kindergarten reading and content.	*See:* L.K.4.a, L.K.4.b
	L.K.4.a	Identify new meanings for familiar words and apply them accurately (e.g., knowing duck is a bird and learning the verb to duck).	• *Differentiated Instruction Cubes* • *Reading Comprehension Cubes*
	L.K.4.b	Use the most frequently occurring inflections and affixes (e.g., -ed, -s, re-, un-, pre-, -ful, -less) as a clue to the meaning of an unknown word.	• Visual, textual or gestural prompts during conversation
	L.K.5	With guidance and support from adults, explore word relationships and nuances in word meanings.	*See:* L.K.5.a, L.K.5.b, L.K.5.c, L.K.5.d
	L.K.5.a	Sort common objects into categories (e.g., shapes, foods) to gain a sense of the concepts the categories represent.	• *3D Feel & Find* • *Mighty Mind* • *All Around Learning Circle Time Activity Set*
	L.K.5.b	Demonstrate understanding of frequently occurring verbs and adjectives by relating them to their opposites (antonyms).	• *Differentiated Instruction Cubes*
	L.K.5.c	Identify real-life connections between words and their use (e.g., note places at school that are colorful).	• *Differentiated Instruction Cubes* • *What Do You Do With It? ConversaCards*
	L.K.5.d	Distinguish shades of meaning among verbs describing the same general action (e.g., walk, march, strut, prance) by acting out the meanings.	• *Differentiated Instruction Cubes* • *I Can Do That! Game*
	L.K.6	Use words and phrases acquired through conversations, reading and being read to, and responding to texts.	• *All Around Learning Circle Time Activity Set* • Classroom reading materials • Visual, textual or gestural prompts during conversation

*Teaching Materials listed in italics are included in the kit; those not italicized are not included and can be found in your classroom.

Mathematics

DOMAIN & CLUSTER	CCSS CODE	STANDARD	TEACHING MATERIALS*
DOMAIN: COUNTING AND CARDINALITY			
Know number names and the count sequence	K.CC.A.1	Count to 100 by ones and by tens.	• *All Around Learning Circle Time Activity Set* • *Unifix Cubes* • *Mathematics with Unifix Cubes*
	K.CC.A.2	Count forward beginning from a given number within the known sequence (instead of having to begin at 1).	• *Differentiated Instruction Cubes* • *All Around Learning Circle Time Activity Set*
	K.CC.A.3	Write numbers from 0 to 20. Represent a number of objects with a written numeral 0-20 (with 0 representing a count of no objects).	• *Writing & Art Kit*
Count to tell the number of objects	K.CC.B.4	Understand the relationship between numbers and quantities; connect counting to cardinality.	*See:* K.CC.B.4.a, K.CC.B.4.b, K.CC.B.4.c
	K.CC.B.4.a	When counting objects, say the number names in the standard order, pairing each object with one and only one number name and each number name with one and only one object.	• *Numbers & Counting Pocket Chart* • *Math Discovery Kit* • *Unifix Cubes*
	K.CC.B.4.b	Understand that the last number name said tells the number of objects counted. The number of objects is the same regardless of their arrangement or the order in which they were counted.	• *Math Discovery Kit* • *Measuring Worms* • *Unifix Cubes*
	K.CC.B.4.c	Understand that each successive number name refers to a quantity that is one larger.	• *Math Discovery Kit* • *Unifix Cubes* • *Mathematics with Unifix Cubes*
	K.CC.B.5	Count to answer "how many?" questions about as many as 20 things arranged in a line, a rectangular array, or a circle, or as many as 10 things in a scattered configuration; given a number from 1-20, count out that many objects.	• *Math Discovery Kit* • *Following Auditory Directions* • *Numbers & Counting Pocket Chart* • *Unifix Cubes* • *Mathematics with Unifix Cubes*
Compare numbers	K.CC.C.6	Identify whether the number of objects in one group is greater than, less than, or equal to the number of objects in another group, e.g., by using matching and counting strategies.	• *Math Discovery Kit* • *Unifix Cubes* • *Mathematics with Unifix Cubes* • *Measuring Worms*
	K.CC.C.7	Compare two numbers between 1 and 10 presented as written numerals.	• *Math Discovery Kit* • *Differentiated Instruction Cubes* • *Numbers & Counting Pocket Chart* • *All Around Learning Circle Time Activity Set* • *Unifix Cubes* • *Mathematics with Unifix Cubes*

*Teaching Materials listed in italics are included in the kit; those not italicized are not included and can be found in your classroom.

Mathematics

DOMAIN & CLUSTER	CCSS CODE	STANDARD	TEACHING MATERIALS*
DOMAIN: OPERATIONS AND ALGEBRAIC THINKING			
Understand addition, and understand subtraction	K.OA.A.1	Represent addition and subtraction with objects, fingers, mental images, drawings*, sounds (e.g., claps), acting out situations, verbal explanations, expressions, or equations. *Drawings need not show details, but should show the mathematics in the problem. (This applies wherever drawings are mentioned in the Standards.)	• *Measuring Worms* • *Inchimals* • *Math Discovery Kit* • *Unifix Cubes*
	K.OA.A.2	Solve addition and subtraction word problems, and add and subtract within 10, e.g., by using objects or drawings to represent the problem.	• *Numbers & Counting Pocket Chart* • *Measuring Worms* • *Math Discovery Kit* • *Unifix Cubes*
	K.OA.A.3	Decompose numbers less than or equal to 10 into pairs in more than one way, e.g., by using objects or drawings, and record each decomposition by a drawing or equation (e.g., 5 = 2 + 3 and 5 = 4 + 1).	• *Unifix Cubes* • *Mathematics with Unifix Cubes*
	K.OA.A.4	For any number from 1 to 9, find the number that makes 10 when added to the given number, e.g., by using objects or drawings, and record the answer with a drawing or equation.	• *Inchimals* • *Numbers & Counting Pocket Chart* • *Unifix Cubes*
	K.OA.A.5	Fluently add and subtract within 5.	• *All Around Learning Circle Time Activity Set* • *Math Discovery Kit* • *Inchimals* • *Numbers & Counting Pocket Chart*
DOMAIN: NUMBER AND OPERATIONS IN BASE TEN			
Work with numbers 11-19 to gain foundations for place value	K.NBT.A.1	Compose and decompose numbers from 11 to 19 into ten ones and some further ones, e.g., by using objects or drawings, and record each composition or decomposition by a drawing or equation (such as 18 = 10 + 8); understand that these numbers are composed of ten ones and one, two, three, four, five, six, seven, eight, or nine ones.	• *Unifix Cubes* • *Inchimals*

*Teaching Materials listed in italics are included in the kit; those not italicized are not included and can be found in your classroom.

Mathematics

DOMAIN & CLUSTER	CCSS CODE	STANDARD	TEACHING MATERIALS*
DOMAIN: MEASUREMENT AND DATA			
Describe and compare measurable attributes	K.MD.A.1	Describe measurable attributes of objects, such as length or weight. Describe several measurable attributes of a single object.	• *Measuring Worms* • *Inchimals* • *3D Feel and Find* • *Unifix Cubes* • *Mathematics with Unifix Cubes*
	K.MD.A.2	Directly compare two objects with a measurable attribute in common, to see which object has "more of"/"less of" the attribute, and describe the difference. For example, directly compare the heights of two children and describe one child as taller/shorter.	• *Inchimals* • *Measuring Worms* • *3D Feel & Find* • *Unifix Cubes* • *Mathematics with Unifix Cubes* • *Following Auditory Directions*
Classify objects and count the number of objects in each category	K.MD.B.3	Classify objects into given categories; count the numbers of objects in each category and sort the categories by count.* *Limit category counts to be less than or equal to 10.	• *Mighty Mind* • *Measuring Worms* • *3D Feel & Find*
DOMAIN: GEOMETRY			
Identify and describe shapes	K.G.A.1	Describe objects in the environment using names of shapes, and describe the relative positions of these objects using terms such as above, below, beside, in front of, behind, and next to.	• *I Can Do That! Game* • *Following Auditory Directions*
	K.G.A.2	Correctly name shapes regardless of their orientations or overall size.	• *Mighty Mind* • *All Around Learning Circle Time Activity Set*
	K.G.A.3	Identify shapes as two-dimensional (lying in a plane, "flat") or three-dimensional ("solid").	• *3D Feel and Find* • Drawings of 2D shapes • Classroom books that include 2D shapes
Analyze, compare, create, and compose shapes	K.G.B.4	Analyze and compare two- and three-dimensional shapes, in different sizes and orientations, using informal language to describe their similarities, differences, parts (e.g., number of sides and vertices/"corners") and other attributes (e.g., having sides of equal length).	• *All Around Learning Circle Time Activity Set* • *Mighty Mind*
	K.G.B.5	Model shapes in the world by building shapes from components (e.g., sticks and clay balls) and drawing shapes.	• Clay, toothpicks, straws, and other building materials
	K.G.B.6	Compose simple shapes to form larger shapes. For example, "Can you join these two triangles with full sides touching to make a rectangle?"	• *Mighty Mind*

*Teaching Materials listed in italics are included in the kit; those not italicized are not included and can be found in your classroom.

How To Use This Curriculum

COMMON CORE STATE STANDARDS AND SPECIAL EDUCATION

The adoption of the Common Core State Standards has been a matter of constant debate since its introduction. While the Common Care State Standards are somewhat ambiguous with respect to students with special needs, the fact remains that teachers across the nation are required to implement these standards with limited or no access to effective teaching tools for doing so.

The standards include a 2-page document entitled "Application to Students with Disabilities," which states that "students with disabilities are a heterogeneous group… therefore, *how* these standards are taught and assessed is of the utmost importance in reaching this diverse group of students" (www.corestandards.org/assets/CCSSonSWD-AT.pdf). It uses optimistic language about providing "an historic opportunity to improve access to rigorous academic content standards for students with disabilities."

But many special education teachers are not feeling so optimistic. While access to the standards themselves is available, instruction on how to help our students actually meet the standards is negligible. "Application to Students with Disabilities" briefly mentions that Universal Design for Learning (UDL), instructional accommodations, and assistive technology devices should be used to implement standards, but provides no guidance for what this actually looks like in the classroom. It suggests making accommodations without changing the standards, a suggestion that ignores the individual needs of many of our students.

The Common Core addresses the idea that we need to rigorously prepare ALL students for a successful college and work experience. However, many challenges that we face in special education are not addressed at all, such as the need to teach daily living skills and social skills. These fundamental skills are essential for meeting the goal of the Common Core.

And the goal is a good one. We want our students to be held to high standards, we want to teach them at the edge of their abilities, and we want to provide access to opportunities such as college and meaningful careers, but we need to address the underlying prerequisite skills that make that a

tenable goal. Acknowledging that "*how* these standards are taught and assessed is of the utmost importance" but neglecting to provide resources and tools to teach and assess is counterproductive to attaining these goals.

This guide aims to address the gap in resources: Equipping you with a companion curriculum that specifically addresses the learning needs of students with autism and other special needs, providing resources and teaching strategies for target skills in both ELA and Math, and supplying tips for generalization. This guide utilizes the principles of Applied Behavior Analysis (ABA), an evidence-based practice, to implement the Common Core Standards for kindergarten. While we have included teaching materials in the kit, the targets stand alone, allowing you to use a wide range of materials and supplies that you already have in your classroom.

APPLIED BEHAVIOR ANALYSIS

Applied Behavior Analysis, or ABA, is an empirically proven treatment method for working with individuals with autism and related disorders. Founded in B.F. Skinner's studies of behavior, it focuses on the use of motivation to help individuals achieve their full potential. For decades, ABA has been used to teach a wide range of skills to learners with developmental disabilities.

In 1987, O. Ivar Lovaas published a groundbreaking study about using ABA for young children with autism (Lovaas, 1987; McEachin, Smith, & Lovaas, 1993). "Each of the children in this early intensive intervention project had received several hundred tailored treatment programs and made major and lasting gains in intellectual, social, emotional, and educational skills. Further, nine of the children showed no diagnosable autism at the end of treatment, and eight of those maintained their typical functioning throughout elementary school" (Larsson & Wright, 2011).

While ABA is frequently associated with treating Autism Spectrum Disorders, the principles of ABA can be used to improve the quality of education for any child. Studies have shown that ABA has resulted in positive outcomes for individuals with Down Syndrome, intellectual disabilities, and developmental delays, as well as with individuals who exhibit maladaptive behaviors. ABA consists of many strategies that can be incredibly effective in any classroom that contains students with special needs. Below I have outlined a few of these strategies and provided information about how they relate to the materials contained in this kit.

Data Collection

Data collection should be an essential part of any teaching methodology, and is the very foundation of ABA. Taking data daily and graphing the information makes it possible to quickly see when your student is making progress and when you need to make a change in your teaching procedure. Your school or organization may have a required format for compiling and graphing data. However, we have included reproducible data sheets and graphing sheets for both individuals and for group work, as well as completed samples in Appendix D.

Prior to taking data on a student's progress, it's essential to get baseline data, or information about your student's current level of ability for that skill. Your school will likely have its own methods for attaining and recording baseline data. It is important that you take baseline data on more than one day to avoid making incorrect assumptions. For example, you may state that your student does not know the skill if you only assess the skill on one day in which he happened to have slept little the previous night. Or you may overestimate you student's skill level if you only ask one question and he happens to guess correctly.

For students in special education, it is especially important to maintain skills once they have been mastered. Maintenance is the ability to continue performing the skill after intensive teaching has been completed. I have found it helpful to create index cards with mastered skills written so I can quickly go through maintenance tasks during classroom time. For example, an index card might say "names the letter 'A'" or "counts up to three objects." Failure to maintain previously mastered skills may result in the student losing those skills, thus requiring you to take time to reteach.

There are several methods for taking and displaying data. Here are brief descriptions of the most common types of data you may collect and when to use them.

Per Opportunity is a simple type of data collection that is used to record a student's performance on a task you are teaching. Each time the student has an opportunity to respond to the target demand, record a Yes (Y) or No (N). At the completion of the lesson, calculate the percentage of correct responses. If you are working with a group of students, use the *Per Opportunity Group Data Sheet*; if you are working with a student one-on-one, use the *Per Opportunity Individual Data Sheet* included in Appendix D.

Single-Probe is another form of data you can collect to record student progress in attaining new target skills. Record a plus (+) or minus (-) for only the first possible opportunity a student has to respond to a target demand. Though you only record data for the first possible opportunity, you provide multiple opportunities to practice the skill. If the student responds correctly on three consecutive days, the skill is considered mastered. On the one hand, this method can be beneficial for classroom teachers because the data collection is more manageable, but it does not provide as much information as Per Opportunity data.

ABC Data is used to determine the function of a student's behavior. It is a simple chart you can easily create that is divided into four columns:

- Date/time

- Antecedent — what happens directly before the behavior

- Behavior — what happened, described in a way that is *observable* (i.e., "dropped to the floor and screamed" instead of "tantrummed") and *measureable* (i.e., "screamed for 5 minutes")

- Consequence — what happened directly following the behavior (i.e., "student removed from room" or "teacher went to student's desk and helped him with the math problem")

A pattern may emerge in the consequence column, providing information about what is maintaining the behavior. For example, if you find that following most undesirable behaviors, the student is removed from the class, it is likely that this "time out" is maintaining the behavior.

How To Use This Curriculum

Time Sampling is "a measurement of the presence or absence of behavior within specific time intervals" (Cooper et al., 2007). Time sampling is an effective way to collect data on continuous or high-rate behaviors. It is especially useful for behaviors that do not have a clear beginning or end, such as humming or repetitive behaviors. For time sampling, it's helpful to use a *MotivAider*, a simple electronic device that silently vibrates at timed intervals. It can be programmed to vibrate on a fixed or variable schedule at different duration and intensity levels. It allows you to collect data you otherwise wouldn't be able to while teaching because you don't have to keep an eye on the clock.

Task Analysis is used to collect accurate data for multi-step tasks. Break a larger task into smaller steps and record a plus (+) or minus (–) for the student's independent response to each step within the larger task. You can then divide the number the student completed successfully by the total number of steps to attain a percentage for correct responding for the total task. Task Analysis is frequently used for functional living skills such as washing hands or making a snack. You will find both a blank and a completed Task Analysis in Appendix D to further guide you.

Tips for Managing Data Collection in the Classroom Setting

All of the data that you collect can be used to make teaching decisions, as well as to accurately report information on Individualized Education Plans (IEPs), quarterly progress reports, and in annual reviews. Many teachers struggle with data collection in the classroom setting but it's not as difficult as it may seem to take data and maintain student attention in a busy classroom. Here are a few tips to help you take accurate data:

- Attach the *Per Opportunity Group Data Sheet* to a clipboard to take data on target skills during a small group lesson. It's easier to track data if you're only managing ONE page of information.

- Use tools such as a tally counter to take data for one student during a lesson. A small counter is great because you can put yarn through it and wear it around your neck.

- Place an address label or sticker on your pants or arm. You can mark tallies with a pen there as you teach without having to carry a clipboard or other materials.

- For some lessons, it may be challenging to take the data you need while teaching. Utilize your paraprofessional or assistant teachers. Give clear instructions on the target skill and what type of data you are seeking.

- Consider having your students help with data. You can have them put checkmarks or stickers in a box on an index card when you instruct them to. Collect the index cards at the end of the lesson to record the data.

- Keep it simple! Don't try to take too much data, as it will increase likelihood of errors. Consider simple yes/no data.

- Analyze your data! Your data is meaningless if you don't use it.

Definitions of Procedure and Mastery Criterion

Now that you understand the importance of data and how to take it in the classroom setting, let's take a look at what you do with that data. For each program that you are working on with your student, you should be taking daily data. The procedure for collecting that data and criterion for mastery are described in detail below.

Procedure & Data Collection

An opportunity—also called a trial—refers to a single opportunity to respond to the target question. For "Per Opportunity" data, you should record a 'Y' for a correct response and an 'N' for an incorrect response, prompted response, or no response. Divide the number of correct responses by the total number of opportunities, and you will have a percentage of correct responses, which can then be graphed on the *Per Opportunity Graph* in Appendix D. Per opportunity data can be collected in 1:1 teaching or in small group teaching. Appendix D contains both a *Per Opportunity Individual Data Sheet* and a *Per Opportunity Group Data Sheet*.

Mastery Criterion

Mastery criterion for Per Opportunity data is listed as 80% across three consecutive sessions with two different instructors. There is a *Per Opportunity Graph* in Appendix D for you to complete based on your needs. For example, there are rare instances in which you might want a student to have 100% accuracy, such as looking both ways before crossing the street or urinating in the toilet. You may also be in a teaching environment in which you don't have access to a second instructor, so your mastery criterion may be set for 80% across three consecutive sessions with one instructor. For the purposes of data collection in this curriculum kit, we have set mastery at 80%.

Preference Assessment

Conducting a Preference Assessment for each student should be one of the first things you do when you start teaching a student. You can find a complete *Preference Assessment* in Appendix A. Having a clear understanding of what items and activities are highly motivating for your student will provide opportunities to reinforce correct responses and adaptive behavior.

Having preferred items and activities available has several benefits:

1. It makes it easier for you to reinforce your student for correct responding and desirable behaviors.

2. It pairs you with preferred items, making teaching sessions more positive for the student.

3. It increases opportunities for the learner to request items because he/she will be more motivated to request the preferred items and activities you have made available.

To conduct a Preference Assessment, place many toys and objects within reach of the student and watch how he/she interacts with them for about 20-30 minutes. If you have a learner with poor scanning skills, you can present items two at a time and see what the learner reaches for.

Make several presentations of items to the student, arranging them in different groupings over the course of one session. As you are observing, make tally marks in the appropriate category on the *Preference Assessment* form to easily recognize patterns. When you have completed the assessment, fill in the final page to have a comprehensive list of reinforcing items and activities on record for that student. Conducting a Preference Assessment allows you to fully explore a range of potential items and activities, and also serves to remove your own bias. For example, not all kids are most motivated by the iPad; some kids may actually be most motivated by doing math flashcards.

When beginning a new session or lesson, you may want to informally assess your student's preferences. You can do this by simply asking, "What do you want to play with/ work for today?" or by placing items within reach and seeing what the student reaches for first.

Finally, it is important for you to get parent input. They may be aware of preferred items and activities that you had not previously considered. Parent reporting is also included in the *Preference Assessment* in Appendix A.

Pairing

If you are familiar with ABA, you have probably heard of the term "pairing." The idea behind pairing is that you will establish and maintain a positive relationship with the student by pairing yourself with preferred items or activities (yet another reason the Preference Assessment is so important). Pairing also helps maintain the relationship, prevent boredom, and increase motivation throughout your relationship with the student.

Before each lesson, you should engage in "pre-session" pairing. This means that you are providing free reinforcers without placing demands. For early learners, you might start off a session with blowing bubbles or playing with a parachute. For older learners, you might start off a session with a game or sharing a book the student enjoys. In the classroom, this might include singing a favorite song or giving high-fives as the students take their seats. If possible, it's a good idea to present the students with options during pre-session pairing. Involving choice frequently increases motivation, and it also increases the likelihood of delivering a more highly reinforcing item.

You may feel that pairing every day eats up valuable instructional time. However, pre-session pairing actually serves to increase motivation and cuts down on maladaptive behavior, which increases the amount and the quality of your instructional time for a given lesson (Rispoli et al., 2011).

Variety and novelty are important during pairing as well. A common error is using the same pre-session pairing with every learner. What you believe is reinforcing in general may not be reinforcing for your student in particular. By completing a Preference Assessment, you can avoid this error.

Another common error is using the same pre-session pairing items and activities for every session. A student may love singing "Row Your Boat" one session, and then have no interest the next session. Or, what I see much more often, the learner may love singing "Row Your Boat" every day for two months, and then suddenly has no interest in it. The teacher has depended too heavily on this one preferred activity. Then, without a powerful reinforcer to pair with and use throughout the session, the learner displays a drop in motivation and sometimes a correlating increase in maladaptive behaviors.

There's a word for this: *satiation*. Cooper et al. define satiation as: "A decrease in the frequency of operant behavior presumed to be the result of continued contact with or consumption of a reinforcer that has followed the behavior" (2007). Some students you work with may satiate on reinforcers within minutes, while others may prefer to see the same items over and over from session to session. A student's satiation can vary based on many different variables, so you should be prepared to address it.

One way to address this is to choose not to use the same reinforcers during each session. This way, if a battery dies, you run out of stickers, or something breaks, you have not set yourself and your student up for failure. A second way to address satiation is to remove the item or activity while the student is still highly motivated to engage with it, instead of waiting until he or she has lost interest before introducing other choices.

A final consideration is that students with autism and other developmental delays are frequently provided with sensory items that can be stretched, smooshed, or illuminated. While the items are certainly valuable for pairing and for reinforcement, it may be more valuable to engage in activities with the student, such as cause-and-effect toys and games, or physical activities that require your joint involvement.

Pairing is not an activity that can be easily measured, and it's important to recognize that the pairing process is never finished but is an ongoing part of your relationship with each student. When pairing is consistent, specific to students' interests, and involves a variety of items and activities, students will maintain motivation and you will be more easily able to maintain instructional control.

Motivation and Reinforcement

Reinforcement is a much more complicated subject than it initially appears to be. As previously mentioned, it is necessary to complete a Preference Assessment for each child to learn about what they find reinforcing prior to teaching. Here are a few important things to remember about reinforcement:

- Reinforcement should be individualized for your particular student. Some students are highly motivated by light-up toys or movement activities, others by edibles or music. Just because you think it is reinforcing does not mean that it is! If the learner is not engaging with the item by ignoring it, putting it down, or displaying maladaptive behaviors when the item is present, then the item is not reinforcing at that time.

- Reinforcement should be varied as much as possible. You do not want your student to satiate on the one item or activity that you use all the time for reinforcement.

- Reinforcement is most powerful when it is provided within one second of the desired response to the target question. The longer the amount of time between correct responding and reinforcement, the less meaningful the reinforcement, and the less likely your student is to connect reinforcement to the target response. Moreover, it potentially reinforces behavior that may have occurred in the interim.

- Use differential reinforcement. This means that you provide different qualities of reinforcement for different qualities of responses. For example, if your student answers quickly, clearly, and correctly on the first try you can provide a highly preferred reinforcer. But if your student answers correctly with a minimal prompt, you would provide a less preferred reinforcer. This is another time when access to the *Preference Assessment* results form is beneficial for the teacher because it provides a hierarchy of preferred reinforcers.

- You should work to establish new items as reinforcing, broadening the scope of reinforcers over time. Your ultimate goal is that your student becomes reinforced by your teaching materials or by events likely to occur in the natural environment such as playing chase on the playground or having a person smile at them.

How To Use This Curriculum

- In order to prevent satiation, you should try to keep the preference list robust so that you can vary the reinforcement provided. Think about what happens if you're teaching and your student's preferred activity is watching YouTube on a tablet. If you have not worked with a broad range of preferred items and activities, then you're bound to have a very difficult lesson on the day your Wi-Fi isn't working.

- The pace of instruction and delivery of reinforcement should be fast.

Using Motivating Materials and Activities for Teaching

There are two important ways to use motivating materials and activities with your students. The first is to find highly engaging materials for teaching. For each Common Core State Standard, you will find multiple materials and activities in this kit for teaching and generalizing each skill, which increases the likelihood of having motivating materials available for each individual student. For example, for MATH.CONTENT.K.CC.C.6, the standard states that the student will be able to "identify whether the number of objects in one group is greater than, less than,

or equal to the number of objects in another group." You will see that there are four different materials included in this kit that address that skill. If you know your student struggles with this skill, you should start by picking materials that have the highest likelihood of engaging your student. If your student loves building, you may start with the *Unifix Cubes* because they provide an opportunity to stack and assemble.

The second way to use motivating materials is as positive reinforcement for correct responses. Below is an example of what reinforcement might look like for ELA-LITERACY. RL.K.3. The target skill in this example is for the student to identify setting in a story. In the chart below, the target skill is listed in bold. You'll see from the chart that the target skill is interspersed with mastered skills, such as naming items in pictures and identifying the main character. The student's most highly-preferred reinforcers are high-fives, stickers, and playing with puppets. Other reinforcers include singing a song, verbal praise, and squeezing a ball. The teacher refers to the student's *Preference Assessment* results to link reinforcement to the current lesson.

TASK	INSTRUCTOR SAYS	STUDENT RESPONSE	REINFORCEMENT
Identify main character	"Who is the story about?"	"James."	"That's right!"
Identify setting	"Look at the picture. Can you tell me what time of day it is?"	"Is it morning?"	"It is morning!" combined with high five.
Identify setting	"How do you know it is morning?"	"Because he's with his mommy."	No reinforcement: incorrect response, move to prompt
(Repeat) **Identify setting**	"What is James doing that tells you it's the morning?"	"He's eating breakfast."	"Good job."
Identify items in pictures	"What is James eating for breakfast?"	"He's eating eggs."	"That's right."
Identify characters	"Who is James eating breakfast with?"	"His mom."	"Nice work."
Identify setting	"Where is James?"	"He's in the kitchen."	"He is in the kitchen!" Hands student a puppet. Teacher and student pretend to be characters from story with the puppet.

For more information on reinforcement and using it effectively, I suggest having a look at *The NEW ABA Program Companion* by J. Tyler Fovel, M.A., BCBA.

How To Use This Curriculum

Discriminative Stimulus

Throughout this curriculum you will find the abbreviation 'Sd,' which stands for *discriminative stimulus*. Cooper et al. (2007) define discriminative stimulus as "a stimulus in the presence of which responses of some type have been reinforced and in the absence of which the same type of responses have occurred and not been reinforced." To put it in other terms, the *Sd* is what you say or do to evoke a response that you will reinforce. For example, when teaching a child to respond to "What is your name?" you may give them a high five, verbal praise, or other reinforcement when they respond correctly. The *Sd* in that example is your statement "What is your name?" For each program in the curriculum, we have provided several examples of an *Sd* so you are able to vary it, therefore decreasing the potential for rote responding.

Prompting

When teaching new skills, you may find that your student requires prompts. "A prompt is assistance given by the teacher to promote correct responding" (Leaf & McEachin, 1999). It is important to systematically fade prompts to avoid "prompt dependence" which is when a learner requires a prompt from a teacher or parent in order to complete a task.

There are many different ways to prompt which can be divided into levels according to how intrusive the prompt is. Below is a prompt hierarchy, with the least intrusive prompt at the top and the most intrusive prompt at the bottom. Your goal is to quickly progress through the prompt levels to move your learner to independence.

PROMPTING HIERARCHY

Natural Cue/Independence
Visual Prompt
Verbal Prompt
Gestural Prompt
Modeling
Partial Physical Prompt
Full Physical Prompt

least ↑
most ↓

Research indicates that most-to-least prompting is most effective to teach new skills, whereas least-to-most prompting is preferred for maintaining skills the student has already learned. This means that when teaching a new skill, you would start at the most intrusive prompt, a full physical prompt, and then move your way up the prompt hierarchy until your learner achieves independence with the task.

In order to decrease the possibility of prompt dependence, you should try to quickly move up the prompt hierarchy in a way that makes sense for the skill you are trying to teach. Below are some tips to help you help your learners achieve independence:

- Follow the rule of three: Once your learner has successfully responded to a question three times consecutively, move to a less intrusive prompt.

- If you are taking data, make a notation of what prompt level you are using at each step. And remember: only independent responses should be counted towards the learner's percentage of correct responses.

- At the end of a session or group of trials, note what prompt level you were at by the end of the session. Then start at that level during the next session.

- If your learner does not respond correctly when you move to a less intrusive prompt, then move back to the most recent prompt level. Once they respond again correctly at that prompt level three times consecutively, move again to a less intrusive prompt.

- It's important to note that while verbal prompts are less intrusive than many other types of prompts, they are the most difficult to fade. Though they are less intrusive, you should avoid using them when possible.

- Write down what the prompt levels will look like for the specific task you are teaching in advance. This way you will be fully prepared to quickly move your learner towards independence.

- Differentiate your reinforcement! If you move to a less intrusive prompt and the learner responds correctly, then you should immediately provide a stronger reinforcer than you did for previous responses. If a learner spontaneously responds without a prompt, you should do what I call "throwing them a party" by combining reinforcers (such as tickles and high fives) or by providing a highly desirable reinforcer.

How To Use This Curriculum

• You can pair prompts and then fade out the more intrusive prompts. In the example of pulling up pants in the table below, you can pair a visual prompt with a gestural prompt by showing the symbol for pulling up pants while pointing at the pants. Over time, you stop using the gestural prompt and just use the symbol. You can fade the symbol by systematically making it smaller or fainter.

Below are two different examples illustrating each prompt level from least-to-most intrusive. In the first column, you'll find the prompt level. In the example given in the second column, the goal is for the learner to greet a person who walks into the room. In the example in the third column, the goal is for the learner to pull up his/her pants after using the bathroom as a part of a toileting routine.

PROMPT LEVEL	GREETING	PULLING UP PANTS
Natural Cue/Independence	Learner says "Hello" upon seeing person enter room.	Learner pulls up pants immediately after flushing or after wiping (whichever step is directly before "pulling up pants")
Visual Prompt	It's possible that you may use some sort of textual prompt, then fade the script, such as showing the words "Hello, how are you today?"	You may have symbols or a picture schedule the student uses to remember the steps for toileting.
Verbal Prompt	You say, "Say Hello," then the learner says, "Hello."	You say, "What comes next?" or "Pull up your pants." Then the learner pulls them up without assistance.
Gestural Prompt	You silently point or nod toward the person who has entered the room, then the learner says, "Hello."	You point at the pants, and then the learner pulls them up without assistance.
Modeling	You say "Hello, _____" and wave, then the learner says, "Hello." You may include a prompt such as "Follow me" or "Do what I do."	N/A
Partial Physical Prompt	You might touch the learner's elbow and gently raise his/her hand to begin waving in greeting, and then let him/her finish the wave and say, "Hello."	You may tap or gently press the learner's wrist or elbows towards the floor, and then let him/her finish pulling up his/her pants.
Full Physical Prompt	You pick up the learner's hand and wave it in greeting.	You gently guide the learner's hands to pick up his/her pants, and then guide him/her through the process of pulling them up.

Generalization

Many students with special needs struggle to generalize skills. We must address this in our teaching by ensuring that our students are able to successfully use a skill in all environments, with all people, and with all materials. Here are a few examples of what it may look like when a student has not generalized a skill:

- Has *not* generalized across environments: The student is able to accurately count groups of objects in the classroom but is unable to count out tokens to claim a prize at a fair.

- Has *not* generalized across people: The student will respond to "wh" questions when presented by the teacher during a lesson, but will not respond to "wh" questions when asked a question by the crossing guard on the way to school.

- Has *not* generalized across materials: The student can match pictured items but is unable to match socks when helping with laundry at home.

As you teach, it is essential to build in opportunities for generalization in each lesson. This kit includes materials and other suggestions for generalizing skills. In addition, the *Per Opportunity Graph* in Appendix D provides space for you to note the materials, people, and environments you used for both teaching and generalization to ensure the student is gaining full independence with the target skill.

Generalization Criterion

For each standard, it is important to conduct a generalization probe. This means you will present the demand with novel materials, in a novel environment, or by a novel person. The student has generalized the skill if they respond correctly on the first attempt. Information about your generalization probes can be recorded at the bottom of the *Per Opportunity Graph* in Appendix D. You should also record the date of the generalization probe in the appropriate column on the program pages.

Natural Environment Teaching (NET)

Beyond providing teaching opportunities during lessons individually or in small groups, you will also want to provide opportunities to respond to the target skill in the natural environment. The natural environment may include the playground, the grocery store, interactions with peers during free play, or any other area in which skills would be applied outside of the teaching environment. You should embed teaching targets into play scenarios, games, or activities.

NET is especially important for students with autism and other developmental delays who struggle with generalization. It is not useful for these children to only be capable of completing a task in a teaching session. Planning lessons that utilize skills in the natural environment is essential. For example, if you are working on the Common Core standards in the *Speaking and Listening* strand, it is not useful for a student to only be able to ask questions at the table in the classroom. Creating opportunities for students to be taught how to ask questions in the community, in stores, or during play is an important part of the teaching process.

CONSIDERATIONS AND RESOURCES RELATED TO LANGUAGE DEVELOPMENT

The Common Core State Standards include many requirements for students to share thoughts, speak in grammatically correct sentences, and provide appropriate conversational responses. While these expectations may be developmentally appropriate for their same-age peers, teaching language out of developmental order can have long-lasting counterproductive effects. For this reason, it is important to assess and understand each student's developmental skill in the area of language, then teach to their individual needs.

For additional information you should visit the website www.corestandards.org. The site includes detailed information about each standard, as well as research related to how the standards were made. For ELA standards, we highly recommend that you look at the Test Exemplars and Sample Performance Tasks found at www.corestandards.org/assets/Appendix_B.pdf, a document that provides dozens of suggested texts for a range of standards. This can be especially helpful as you are choosing appropriate reading materials for meeting the standards with your individual students.

As a special education teacher, if you are working with children with autism or severe language delays, you should be aware of the stages of language development, assess your student's language ability, and set appropriate goals for the best long-term benefits of that student. *The Verbal Behavior Milestones Assessment and Placement Program* (VB-MAPP) by Mark Sundberg, PhD, is an excellent tool for assessing and setting goals for your students.

You can also utilize Brown's Stages of Language Development. It's important to note that while Brown lists the approximate ages that most children develop these language skills, it is essential to teach to the current *developmental stage* your student is in, and not their *chronological age*. You can find a sample of the Stages of Language Development at www.education.com/reference/article/acquisition-sentence-forms.

After you have assessed, you should refer to Appendix B, *Encouraging Social Interactions and Conversations*, for guidance on supporting your student at their current level of language development. This appendix provides suggestions for encouraging mands, as well as multiple examples of mands you can teach in the classroom environment. It will also provide examples of leading statements you can make to promote the skill of asking questions.

Frequently, teachers may feel pressure from parents, administrators, or other staff to teach language skills that are well above an individual student's current level of functioning. This can produce serious problems in the student's communication skills. For example, if you have a student who is in Stage 1 of Brown's Stages of Language Development, but you are requiring them to use full sentences to communicate, it's likely that they will not comprehend all of the words in the sentence. You may see errors such as these:

Teacher: What should I do?
Student: I want throw please.

Teacher: Do you want to draw or listen to music?
Student: Give me draw please.

While it may take much longer for our students to move through the stages than their typically developing peers, it is important that we meet them at their current skill level.

If you teach well above their current skill level, research shows that they do not acquire full comprehension of basic language, misuse common words, and/or plateau in their language development.

There are several special considerations a teacher must make when choosing how to practice communication effectively with students. Below I've outlined some common obstacles and potential teaching methods for addressing them.

Concern: When teaching language with discrete trials, it is possible that students may become prompt dependent and fail to initiate conversation on their own or participate in novel conversation.
Teaching Method: Utilize paraprofessionals, teaching assistants, and parents when possible to teach conversation. One adult should be the conversation partner who will discuss highly motivating topics with the student. The other adult will be responsible for all prompts. This way, the conversation maintains a natural form and cadence since one adult is solely responsible for prompting and doesn't have to converse.

Concern: For students who are not yet speaking, you need to provide opportunities for teaching the concept of social exchanges.
Teaching Method: You may use tools such as sign language, Picture Exchange Communication System, or an augmentative/alternative communication device.

Concern: Some students may struggle greatly with basic aspects of communication such as eye contact and orienting their body towards the conversation partner.
Teaching Method: These students need to be reinforced for these behaviors to increase the future frequency. For example, when a student makes eye contact, you can provide reinforcement such as high fives, silly faces or sounds, or access to tangibles. More importantly, communication and conversation should be individualized for each student, and it should be FUN! You can increase your student's interest by engaging them with activities and topics they are motivated by, using materials that encourage active play, and planning breaks as needed.

Concern: For students struggling with communication, it's important to recognize that as a teacher, a pattern of reinforcing being quiet and waiting for instruction may actually decrease spontaneous vocalizations (Sundberg & Partington, 1999, pp. 139–156).

Teaching Method: Focus on reinforcing spontaneous vocalizations and babbling. Consider using activity schedules as a visual prompt for a learner to initiate a social interaction (McClannahan & Kranz, 2005, pp. 10–11).

While it is important to provide rigorous academic programs for our students, the unique concerns listed above make implementation of the Common Core State Standards challenging. The "Application for Students with Disabilities" discusses providing "meaningful access" to the standards. If we teach well above a student's current skill level, we are not providing meaningful access. Because this is a kindergarten kit, it's not possible to drill down any further into the Common Core. We recommend that you assess using the VB-MAPP if it is clear that a particular student is not yet developmentally ready to learn the standards. While your school may require you to use a different assessment (such as the SANDI), it is still useful to complete the VB-MAPP because it provides an accurate portrait of your student's current skill level and barriers to learning, as well as makes recommendations for appropriate IEP goals.

Below is a list of some possible signs that you may be teaching above your student's current skill level:

- The student masters a goal when taught in discrete trials, but has not mastered the prerequisite skills.

- After the student masters a skill, he/she is not able to maintain it if it is practiced with lower frequency.

- The student masters a skill but is unable to respond accurately when it is intermixed with other mastered skills.

- The student is unable to generalize the skill after mastery.

- The student is not mastering any of the material that you are teaching.

- The student is mastering one skill at a much slower rate than he/she typically masters skills.

It is absolutely imperative that you meet each student at his/her current skill level, even if that means you do not start with the CCSS. However, the use of the CCSS provides guidelines for the overall scope of what we want our students to learn, and it provides teaching opportunities within each standard.

How to Use This Kit

PUTTING IT ALL TOGETHER

This kit is specifically designed to address the English Language Arts and Math goals in the Common Core State Standards **for students in special education**. Each standard is broken down into small, teachable steps to help track student progress to make the CCSS accessible for students with special needs.

Each strand has an overview page denoting the standards, kit materials, additional classroom materials and activities, and a tip for generalization. This is followed by individual pages for each Common Core State Standard enabling you to take data on when the target was introduced, mastered and generalized directly on the page for each student. The standard pages also provide detailed information on teaching procedure, how to use the materials in that particular lesson, along with the discriminative stimulus used for that target skill.

You should start by exploring the teaching materials contained within the kit. Think about how you might use them to meet your students' current needs. Ask yourself:

· What might be highly motivating for each student?

· What materials would be best for independent work? Group work?

· Are there any materials that might be aversive to particular students?

· What areas of the classroom would be best for setting up or storing these materials?

· How can I use the materials in conjunction with the materials I already have in the classroom?

Once you're comfortable with the scope of the materials, familiarize yourself with the curriculum book and how each standard is organized. Every page in this kit is designed to be reproducible for each student in your classroom. Everything you need to teach and record information about student progress is contained within this book and can be taught with the included kit materials. However, the targets can also be used independently with any teaching materials or activities that may be appropriate for a particular student.

We have intentionally selected materials for this kit to mutually support different targets. While we highlight one or two specific materials explained in depth in the Teaching Procedure, we also list additional kit materials that can be used to teach, maintain or generalize the target skills in each program.

While we do our best to include the exact products described in the Teaching Procedure, there may be rare occasions when a product is unavailable for an extended period of time or has been suddenly discontinued. In these cases, we will substitute the product with one of equal purpose and value that you can still use for the Teaching Procedure described.

The sample pages that follow will serve as a User Guide to the salient information presented on each Strand and Standard page.

Strand Reference Page

Brief description of the skill set addressed in this strand.

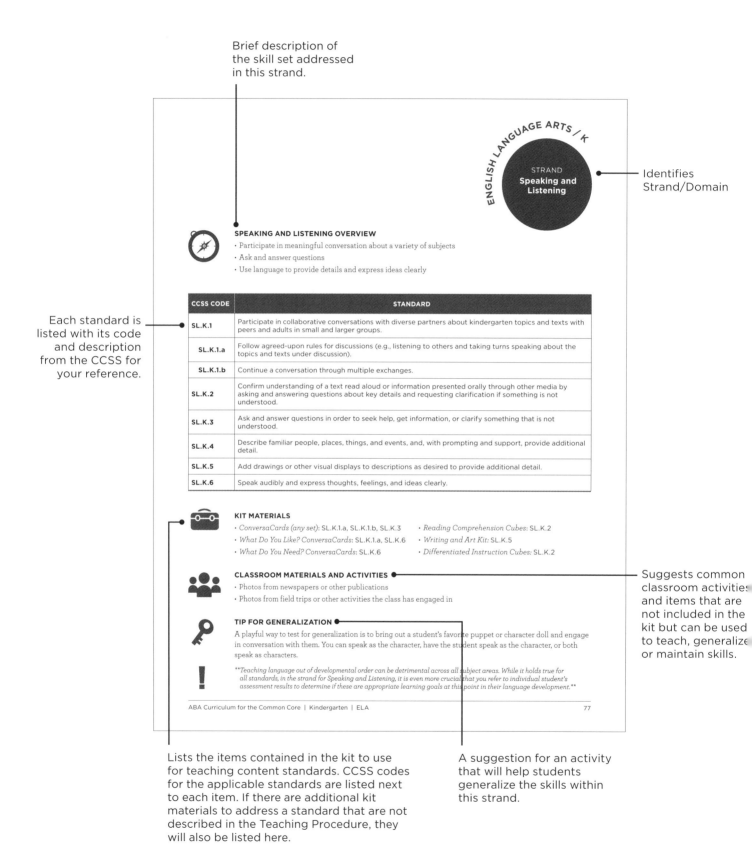

ENGLISH LANGUAGE ARTS / K

STRAND
Speaking and Listening

Identifies Strand/Domain

SPEAKING AND LISTENING OVERVIEW
· Participate in meaningful conversation about a variety of subjects
· Ask and answer questions
· Use language to provide details and express ideas clearly

Each standard is listed with its code and description from the CCSS for your reference.

CCSS CODE	STANDARD
SL.K.1	Participate in collaborative conversations with diverse partners about kindergarten topics and texts with peers and adults in small and larger groups.
SL.K.1.a	Follow agreed-upon rules for discussions (e.g., listening to others and taking turns speaking about the topics and texts under discussion).
SL.K.1.b	Continue a conversation through multiple exchanges.
SL.K.2	Confirm understanding of a text read aloud or information presented orally through other media by asking and answering questions about key details and requesting clarification if something is not understood.
SL.K.3	Ask and answer questions in order to seek help, get information, or clarify something that is not understood.
SL.K.4	Describe familiar people, places, things, and events, and, with prompting and support, provide additional detail.
SL.K.5	Add drawings or other visual displays to descriptions as desired to provide additional detail.
SL.K.6	Speak audibly and express thoughts, feelings, and ideas clearly.

KIT MATERIALS
· *ConversaCards (any set)*: SL.K.1.a, SL.K.1.b, SL.K.3
· *What Do You Like? ConversaCards*: SL.K.1.a, SL.K.6
· *What Do You Need? ConversaCards*: SL.K.6
· *Reading Comprehension Cubes*: SL.K.2
· *Writing and Art Kit*: SL.K.5
· *Differentiated Instruction Cubes*: SL.K.2

CLASSROOM MATERIALS AND ACTIVITIES
· Photos from newspapers or other publications
· Photos from field trips or other activities the class has engaged in

Suggests common classroom activities and items that are not included in the kit but can be used to teach, generalize or maintain skills.

TIP FOR GENERALIZATION
A playful way to test for generalization is to bring out a student's favorite puppet or character doll and engage in conversation with them. You can speak as the character, have the student speak as the character, or both speak as characters.

Teaching language out of developmental order can be detrimental across all subject areas. While it holds true for all standards, in the strand for Speaking and Listening, it is even more crucial that you refer to individual student's assessment results to determine if these are appropriate learning goals at this point in their language development.

ABA Curriculum for the Common Core | Kindergarten | ELA

77

Lists the items contained in the kit to use for teaching content standards. CCSS codes for the applicable standards are listed next to each item. If there are additional kit materials to address a standard that are not described in the Teaching Procedure, they will also be listed here.

A suggestion for an activity that will help students generalize the skills within this strand.

Standard Reference Page

These sheets can be reproduced for each student to track progress on each standard. Supplemental daily data sheets can be found in Appendix D.

This header notes the Strand, Cluster, and the Standards included for easy reference.

The kit materials described in the Teaching Procedure are marked in bold. Other materials included in the kit that can be used to teach, generalize or maintain the skill are also listed here.

CCSS Standard addressed by this program.

The Teaching Procedure presents one suggestion for how to use the included kit materials to teach the standard.

The discriminative stimulus (or Sd) is what you say or do to evoke a response. Two to three potential Sds are listed for each standard. It is important for long-term learning and generalization to vary the Sd instead of using the same one each time.

Enter the date the target was introduced, mastered, and probed for generalization, along with the initials of the instructor.

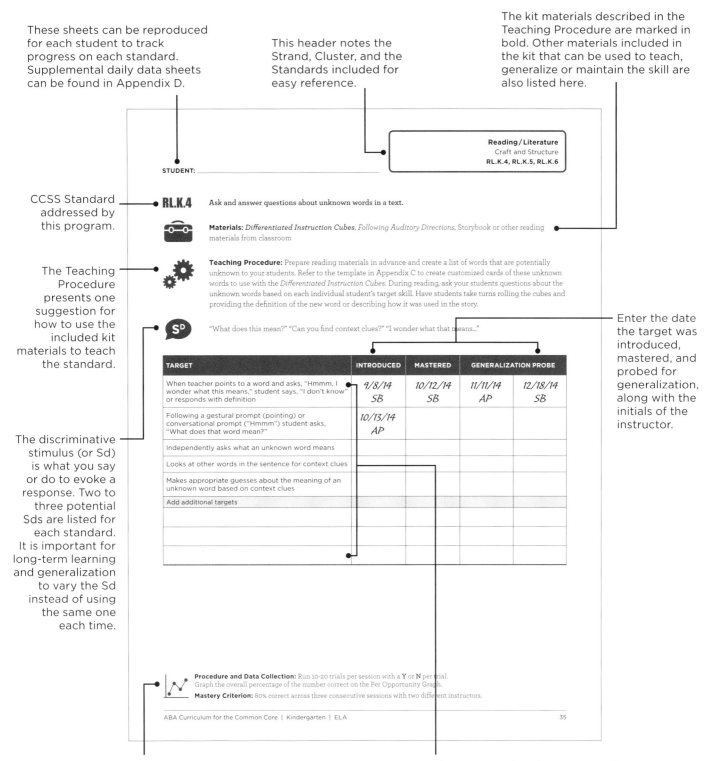

Reading/Literature
Craft and Structure
RL.K.4, RL.K.5, RL.K.6

STUDENT: _____

RL.K.4 Ask and answer questions about unknown words in a text.

Materials: *Differentiated Instruction Cubes, Following Auditory Directions,* Storybook or other reading materials from classroom

Teaching Procedure: Prepare reading materials in advance and create a list of words that are potentially unknown to your students. Refer to the template in Appendix C to create customized cards of these unknown words to use with the *Differentiated Instruction Cubes.* During reading, ask your students questions about the unknown words based on each individual student's target skill. Have students take turns rolling the cubes and providing the definition of the new word or describing how it was used in the story.

Sᴰ "What does this mean?" "Can you find context clues?" "I wonder what that means..."

TARGET	INTRODUCED	MASTERED	GENERALIZATION PROBE	
When teacher points to a word and asks, "Hmmm, I wonder what this means," student says, "I don't know" or responds with definition	9/8/14 SB	10/12/14 SB	11/11/14 AP	12/18/14 SB
Following a gestural prompt (pointing) or conversational prompt ("Hmmm") student asks, "What does that word mean?"	10/13/14 AP			
Independently asks what an unknown word means				
Looks at other words in the sentence for context clues				
Makes appropriate guesses about the meaning of an unknown word based on context clues				
Add additional targets				

Procedure and Data Collection: Run 10-20 trials per session with a **Y** or **N** per trial. Graph the overall percentage of the number correct on the Per Opportunity Graph.
Mastery Criterion: 80% correct across three consecutive sessions with two different instructors.

For simple recordkeeping, information about how many trials to run during a session, as well as criteria that students must meet in order for the skill to be mastered are listed here. All data can be collected on forms provided in Appendix D.

These targets break the standard down into prerequisite steps and skills that your student should master in order to meet the standard. You may need to add additional prerequisite skills to meet the unique needs of an individual student so there are blank boxes for you to add your own targets.

The Big Picture

Our goal with this kit is to supply you with tools to make the Common Core State Standards for ELA and Math accessible to students with special needs by breaking down each standard into teachable steps and providing an ABA framework to increase student success. The materials and information provided in this kit also serve to better prepare you to utilize ABA with all of your students. The evidence-based strategies described here have been proven to have significant impacts on students with autism, as well as a range of other disabilities such as ADHD and Down Syndrome. We hope this kit will allow you to prepare individualized lessons aligned with Common Core State Standards, track student progress effectively, and embrace creativity in your teaching to meet the everyday challenges presented in your classroom.

We wish you the best of luck and success.

LITERATURE OVERVIEW

- Participate in conversations about both familiar and novel texts
- Understand categories of different texts
- Compare and contrast many aspects of texts

CCSS CODE	STANDARD
RL.K.1	With prompting and support, ask and answer questions about key details in the text.
RL.K.2	With prompting and support, retell familiar stories, including key details.
RL.K.3	With prompting and support, identify characters, settings, and major events in a story.
RL.K.4	Ask and answer questions about unknown words in a text.
RL.K.5	Recognize common types of texts (e.g., storybooks, poems).
RL.K.6	With prompting and support, name the author and illustrator of a story and define the role of each in telling the story.
RL.K.7	With prompting and support, describe the relationship between illustrations and the story in which they appear (e.g., what moment in a story an illustration depicts).
RL.K.9	With prompting and support, compare and contrast the adventures and experiences of characters in familiar stories.
RL.K.10	Actively engage in group reading activities with purpose and understanding.

Note: RL.K.8 is not applicable to Literature.

KIT MATERIALS

- *Reading Comprehension Cubes*: RL.K.1, RL.K.2, RL.K.3, RL.K.5, RL.K.6, RL.K.10
- *What Happened? ConversaCards*: RL.K.1, RL.K.2
- *Differentiated Instruction Cubes*: RL.K.1, RL.K.2, RL.K.3, RL.K.4, RL.K.6, RL.K.7, RL.K.10
- *Following Auditory Directions*: RL.K.4
- *All Around Circle Time Activity Set*: RL.K.10

CLASSROOM MATERIALS AND ACTIVITIES

- Classroom reading materials
- Puppets, figurines, or other characters
- Felt cut-outs for retelling familiar stories

TIP FOR GENERALIZATION

Many learners with autism are highly motivated by specific TV shows or cartoons. Utilize their motivation to practice and generalize skills such as identifying character and setting, retelling stories, or comparing and contrasting two episodes of the same show.

STUDENT: _____

RL.K.1

With prompting and support, ask and answer questions about key details in the text.

Materials: *Reading Comprehension Cubes, Differentiated Instruction Cubes, What Happened? ConversaCards,* Storybook from the classroom

Teaching Procedure: Read a classroom book or story with your students and ask questions so students can reference the text and pictures. After the story is complete, let students take turns rolling the *Reading Comprehension Cubes* and responding to questions to check for understanding. If your students cannot independently respond to questions from the *Reading Comprehension Cubes,* refer to the template in Appendix C to create customized cards to use with the *Differentiated Instruction Cubes.* For students who are not yet ready to respond to reading comprehension questions, you should use the *What Happened? ConversaCards* to teach picture comprehension.

"Who is the story about?" "Tell me what happened after _____." "Where did they go?"

TARGET	INTRODUCED	MASTERED	GENERALIZATION PROBE	
Responds to "who" questions about the text				
Responds to "where" questions about the text				
Responds to "what" questions about the text				
When asked, identifies the problem in the story				
When asked, identifies the solution in the story				
Add additional targets				

Procedure and Data Collection: Run 10-20 trials per session with a **Y** or **N** per trial. Graph the overall percentage of the number correct on the Per Opportunity Graph.

Mastery Criterion: 80% correct across three consecutive sessions with two different instructors.

STUDENT: _____

RL.K.2   With prompting and support, retell familiar stories, including key details.

Materials: *Reading Comprehension Cubes, What Happened? ConversaCards, Differentiated Instruction Cubes,* Classroom reading materials

Teaching Procedure: Have students respond to questions about a familiar story from a book previously read in class, a favorite TV show, or real life situation, such as a class field trip. For students who struggle with this skill, you may want to include pictures to prompt their retelling.

"Tell me the story about _____." "Can you share the story with me?"

TARGET	INTRODUCED	MASTERED	GENERALIZATION PROBE	
When asked to retell a familiar story, includes who the story is about				
When asked to retell a familiar story, includes where the story takes place				
When asked to retell a familiar story, includes information about the problem				
When asked to retell a familiar story, includes information about the solution				
Add additional targets				

Procedure and Data Collection: Run 10-20 trials per session with a **Y** or **N** per trial. Graph the overall percentage of the number correct on the Per Opportunity Graph.

Mastery Criterion: 80% correct across three consecutive sessions with two different instructors.

STUDENT: _____

RL.K.3 With prompting and support, identify characters, settings, and major events in a story.

Materials: *Reading Comprehension Cubes*, *Differentiated Instruction Cubes*, Storybook from the classroom

Teaching Procedure: Read a classroom book or story with your students and ask questions so students can reference the text and pictures. After the story is complete, let students take turns rolling the *Reading Comprehension Cubes* and responding to additional questions to check for understanding. If your students cannot independently respond to questions from the *Reading Comprehension Cubes*, refer to the template in Appendix C to create customized cards to use with the *Differentiated Instruction Cubes*.

"Who said _____?" "Where did she find the _____?" "What happened next?"

TARGET	INTRODUCED	MASTERED	GENERALIZATION PROBE	
Identifies main characters in a picture				
Identifies the setting in a picture				
Summarizes what is happening in a picture				
Identifies main characters in a story				
Identifies the setting in a story				
Summarizes what is happening in a story				
Add additional targets				

Procedure and Data Collection: Run 10-20 trials per session with a **Y** or **N** per trial. Graph the overall percentage of the number correct on the Per Opportunity Graph.

Mastery Criterion: 80% correct across three consecutive sessions with two different instructors.

STUDENT: _____

RL.K.4   Ask and answer questions about unknown words in a text.

Materials: *Differentiated Instruction Cubes*, *Following Auditory Directions*, Storybook or other reading materials from classroom

Teaching Procedure: Prepare reading materials in advance and create a list of words that are potentially unknown to your students. Refer to the template in Appendix C to create customized cards of these unknown words to use with the *Differentiated Instruction Cubes*. During reading, ask your students questions about the unknown words based on each individual student's target skill. Have students take turns rolling the cubes and providing the definition of the new word or describing how it was used in the story.

"What does this mean?" "Can you find context clues?" "I wonder what that means…"

TARGET	INTRODUCED	MASTERED	GENERALIZATION PROBE	
When teacher points to a word and asks, "Hmmm, I wonder what this means," student says, "I don't know" or responds with definition				
Following a gestural prompt (pointing) or conversational prompt ("Hmmm") student asks, "What does that word mean?"				
Independently asks what an unknown word means				
Looks at other words in the sentence for context clues				
Makes appropriate guesses about the meaning of an unknown word based on context clues				
Add additional targets				

Procedure and Data Collection: Run 10-20 trials per session with a **Y** or **N** per trial. Graph the overall percentage of the number correct on the Per Opportunity Graph.

Mastery Criterion: 80% correct across three consecutive sessions with two different instructors.

STUDENT: _____

 RL.K.5 Recognize common types of texts (e.g., storybooks, poems).

 Materials: *Reading Comprehension Cubes*, Reading materials from classroom

 Teaching Procedure: Provide characteristics of a specific type of text (e.g., What makes a text a poem?). Then, provide several examples and non-examples. For instance, you may present three familiar fairy tales and two familiar poems on the table and have students identify the fairy tales.

 "What is this?" "Is this a poem or a story?" "Tell me what kind of story this is."

TARGET	INTRODUCED	MASTERED	GENERALIZATION PROBE	
Identifies a text as fiction				
Identifies a poem				
Identifies a biography or true story about a person				
Identifies a fairy tale				
Add additional targets				

Procedure and Data Collection: Run 10-20 trials per session with a **Y** or **N** per trial. Graph the overall percentage of the number correct on the Per Opportunity Graph.

Mastery Criterion: 80% correct across three consecutive sessions with two different instructors.

STUDENT: _____

RL.K.6 With prompting and support, name the author and illustrator of a story and define the role of each in telling the story.

Materials: *Differentiated Instruction Cubes, Reading Comprehension Cubes,* Storybook or other reading materials from classroom

Teaching Procedure: Prior to this activity, create cards for the *Differentiated Instruction Cubes* using the list of questions provided for RL.K.6 in Appendix C. Have multiple storybooks or reading materials visible. Students take turns rolling the cubes and responding to the question for one of the reading materials. Questions about the author and illustrator are also included in the *Reading Comprehension Cubes* if you want to mix those questions in with other questions related to comprehension.

"Who wrote the story?" "What is the author's name?" "What does an author do?"

TARGET	INTRODUCED	MASTERED	GENERALIZATION PROBE	
Identifies the author of a story				
Identifies the illustrator of a story				
Explains the role of an author in telling a story				
Explains the role of an illustrator in telling a story				
Add additional targets				

Procedure and Data Collection: Run 10-20 trials per session with a **Y** or **N** per trial. Graph the overall percentage of the number correct on the Per Opportunity Graph.

Mastery Criterion: 80% correct across three consecutive sessions with two different instructors.

STUDENT: _____

 RL.K.7 With prompting and support, describe the relationship between illustrations and the story in which they appear (e.g., what moment in a story an illustration depicts).

 Materials: *Differentiated Instruction Cubes*, Storybook or other reading materials from classroom

 Teaching Procedure: Prior to this activity, create cards for the *Differentiated Instruction Cubes* using the list of questions provided for RL.K.7 in Appendix C. Read a classroom book or story with your students. After the story is complete, students take turns rolling the *Differentiated Instruction Cubes* and responding to the question for one of the reading materials.

 "Tell me about the picture." "What part of the story is this picture illustrating?" "Tell me what is happening in the story right now."

TARGET	INTRODUCED	MASTERED	GENERALIZATION PROBE	
Describes what is happening in the illustration prior to hearing/reading the text				
References the picture to retell what was read in the text				
Tells how the illustration relates to the text				
Add additional targets				

 Procedure and Data Collection: Run 10-20 trials per session with a **Y** or **N** per trial. Graph the overall percentage of the number correct on the Per Opportunity Graph.

Mastery Criterion: 80% correct across three consecutive sessions with two different instructors.

STUDENT: _____

RL.K.9

With prompting and support, compare and contrast the adventures and experiences of characters in familiar stories.

Materials: Storybook or other reading materials from classroom, index cards, visual prompts (not included in kit)

Teaching Procedure: Read or present two familiar stories. Put visual prompts within sight of students. For instance, show pictures of the main character from each story. Give each student words or pictures on index cards to match to the appropriate character, and prompt conversation by comparing and contrasting the two stories. For instance, index cards could show setting, illustrations from the story, or adjectives describing the characters.

"How is _____'s problem similar to _____'s problem?" "What is different about the story of _____ and the story of _____?" "Tell me how they are similar."

TARGET	INTRODUCED	MASTERED	GENERALIZATION PROBE	
When presented with choices, tells which characters from familiar stories had similar adventures and experiences				
When presented with choices, tells which characters from familiar stories had different adventures and experiences				
Compares and contrasts adventures and experiences of two characters from familiar stories				
Add additional targets				

Procedure and Data Collection: Run 10-20 trials per session with a **Y** or **N** per trial. Graph the overall percentage of the number correct on the Per Opportunity Graph.

Mastery Criterion: 80% correct across three consecutive sessions with two different instructors.

STUDENT: _____

RL.K.10 Actively engage in group reading activities with purpose and understanding.

Materials: *Reading Comprehension Cubes, Differentiated Instruction Cubes, All Around Learning Circle Time Activity Set*, Storybook or other reading materials from classroom

Teaching Procedure: Create a clear routine for starting group reading activities. This can include audio or visual cues that a transition is about to take place. Introduce the group reading activity. Use visual and tactile materials such as puppets when applicable. After the story is complete, let students take turns rolling the *Reading Comprehension Cubes* and responding to questions to check for understanding. If your students cannot independently respond to questions from the *Reading Comprehension Cubes*, refer to the template in Appendix C to create customized cards to use with the *Differentiated Instruction Cubes*.

Presentation of a book. "It's time for circle time." "Can you tell me who the story is about?"

TARGET	INTRODUCED	MASTERED	GENERALIZATION PROBE	
Sits during group reading for five minutes without disruptive behavior				
Sits during group reading for 10 minutes without disruptive behavior				
Attends to group reading activity for five minutes				
Attends to group reading activity for 10 minutes				
Responds to two different group instructions				
Responds to five different group instructions				
Raises hand to respond to a question presented by the teacher				
Responds to three questions presented by the teacher during group reading activity				
Responds to five questions presented by the teacher during group reading activity				
Add additional targets				

Procedure and Data Collection: Run 10-20 trials per session with a **Y** or **N** per trial. Graph the overall percentage of the number correct on the Per Opportunity Graph.

Mastery Criterion: 80% correct across three consecutive sessions with two different instructors.

INFORMATIONAL TEXT OVERVIEW

- Participate in meaningful conversation about informational texts, such as newspapers, photos with captions, graphs, and other nonfiction materials
- Understand the parts of a book as well as the roles of authors and illustrators
- Compare and contrast many aspects of informational texts

CCSS CODE	STANDARD
RI.K.1	With prompting and support, ask and answer questions about key details in a text.
RI.K.2	With prompting and support, identify the main topic and retell key details of a text.
RI.K.3	With prompting and support, describe the connection between two individuals, events, ideas, or pieces of information in a text.
RI.K.4	With prompting and support, ask and answer questions about unknown words in a text.
RI.K.5	Identify the front cover, back cover, and title page of a book.
RI.K.6	Name the author and illustrator of a text and define the role of each in presenting the ideas and information in a text.
RI.K.7	With prompting and support, describe the relationship between illustrations and the text in which they appear (e.g., what person, place, thing, or idea in the text an illustration depicts).
RI.K.8	With prompting and support, identify the reasons an author gives to support points in a text.
RI.K.9	With prompting and support, identify basic similarities in and differences between two texts on the same topic (e.g., in illustrations, descriptions, or procedures).
RI.K.10	Actively engage in reading activities with purpose and understanding.

KIT MATERIALS

- *Reading Comprehension Cubes*: RI.K.1, RI.K.2, RI.K.4, RI.K.6, RI.K.8, RI.K.10
- *Differentiated Instruction Cubes*: RI.K.1, RI.K.2, RI.K.3, RI.K.4, RI.K.5, RI.K.6, RI.K.7, RI.K.8, RI.K.9, RI.K.10
- *What Happened? ConversaCards*: RI.K.2
- *All Around Circle Time Activity Set* : RI.K.10

CLASSROOM MATERIALS AND ACTIVITIES

- Classroom books
- Retelling main idea of favorite TV shows or cartoons

TIP FOR GENERALIZATION

Bring in pictures from newspapers or magazines. Have students describe what they think the story may be about. Depending on the skill level of each student, you may accept one-word responses or full-sentence responses.

STUDENT: _____

RI.K.1   With prompting and support, ask and answer questions about key details in a text.

Materials: *Reading Comprehension Cubes,* *Differentiated Instruction Cubes,* Informational text from the classroom

Teaching Procedure: Read an informational text such as a nonfiction book with your students and ask questions so students can reference the text and pictures. After the reading is complete, let students take turns rolling the *Reading Comprehension Cubes* and responding to additional questions to check for understanding. If your students cannot independently respond to questions from the *Reading Comprehension Cubes*, refer to the template in Appendix C to create customized cards to use with the *Differentiated Instruction Cubes*.

"Who said _____?" "What does the author think about _____?"

TARGET	INTRODUCED	MASTERED	GENERALIZATION PROBE	
Responds to "who" questions about the text				
Responds to "where" questions about the text				
Responds to "what" questions about the text				
Responds with one fact to "What did you learn from the text?"				
Add additional targets				

Procedure and Data Collection: Run 10-20 trials per session with a **Y** or **N** per trial. Graph the overall percentage of the number correct on the Per Opportunity Graph.

Mastery Criterion: 80% correct across three consecutive sessions with two different instructors.

STUDENT: _____

 RI.K.2 With prompting and support, identify the main topic and retell key details of a text.

 Materials: *Reading Comprehension Cubes*, *Differentiated Instruction Cubes*, *What Happened? ConversaCards*, Informational text from the classroom

 Teaching Procedure: Read an informational text such as a nonfiction book with your students and ask questions so students can reference the text and pictures. After reading is complete, let students take turns rolling the *Reading Comprehension Cubes* and responding to questions to check for understanding. If your students cannot independently respond to questions from the *Reading Comprehension Cubes*, refer to the template in Appendix C to create customized cards to use with the *Differentiated Instruction Cubes*. For students who are struggling with reading comprehension, you should consider starting with the *What Happened? ConversaCards* to focus on prerequisite skills.

 "What is the main idea?" "Who is this about?" "Tell me how you know the author feels that way." "Can you give me more information?"

TARGET	INTRODUCED	MASTERED	GENERALIZATION PROBE	
Responds to "What is this mostly about?"				
When provided with the main idea, retells one key detail from the text				
When provided with the main idea, retells three key details from the text				
Retells information from the text including the main idea and key details				
Add additional targets				

Procedure and Data Collection: Run 10-20 trials per session with a **Y** or **N** per trial. Graph the overall percentage of the number correct on the Per Opportunity Graph.

Mastery Criterion: 80% correct across three consecutive sessions with two different instructors.

STUDENT: _____

RI.K.3   With prompting and support, describe the connection between two individuals, events, ideas, or pieces of information in a text.

Materials: *Differentiated Instruction Cubes*, Informational text from the classroom

Teaching Procedure: Prior to the reading activity, prepare the *Differentiated Instruction Cubes* for the text you will be sharing with your students. Refer to the template in Appendix C to create customized cards for teaching this standard. The cards you place in the cubes should relate directly to the text you are reading. For example, one card might have names of two individuals from the story. Read the informational text with your students and ask questions so students can reference the text and pictures. After reading is complete, have students take turns rolling the cubes and sharing the connection between the two individuals, events, ideas, or pieces of information that appear on the cubes.

"What do they have in common?" "What idea do both stories talk about?"

TARGET	INTRODUCED	MASTERED	GENERALIZATION PROBE	
Tells how two individuals from a text are connected to one another				
Tells how two individuals from a novel text are connected to one another				
Tells how two events from a text are connected for three different texts				
Tells how two events from a novel text are connected to one another				
Tells how two pieces of information from a text are connected for three different texts				
Tells how two pieces of information from a novel text are connected to one another				
Tells how two ideas from a text are connected for three different texts				
Tells how two ideas from a novel text are connected to one another				
Add additional targets				

Procedure and Data Collection: Run 10-20 trials per session with a **Y** or **N** per trial. Graph the overall percentage of the number correct on the Per Opportunity Graph.

Mastery Criterion: 80% correct across three consecutive sessions with two different instructors.

STUDENT: _____

 RI.K.4 With prompting and support, ask and answer questions about unknown words in a text.

 Materials: *Reading Comprehension Cubes, Differentiated Instruction Cubes,* Informational text from the classroom

 Teaching Procedure: Prior to the lesson, prepare a list of target words for the text. Read an informational text such as a nonfiction book with your students and ask questions so students can reference the text and pictures. Give students multiple opportunities to define words within the text based on their current skill level. For students who are strong in this area, you can use *Reading Comprehension Cubes* after reading to practice this skill along with other ELA skills. For readers who struggle, you may want to use the *Differentiated Instruction Cubes* and place a target word on each side of the cube. Refer to the template in Appendix C to create customized cards for teaching this standard.

 "I wonder what that means." Pausing to allow for time for the learner to ask. Pointing at the word as a gestural prompt for learner to ask. "Where can we look for clues to the meaning of that word?"

TARGET	INTRODUCED	MASTERED	GENERALIZATION PROBE	
When teacher points to a word and asks, "Hmmm, I wonder what this means," student says, "I don't know" or responds with definition				
Following a gestural prompt (pointing) or conversational prompt ("Hmmm") student asks, "What does that word mean?"				
Independently asks what an unknown word means				
Looks at other words in the sentence for context clues				
Makes appropriate guesses about the meaning of an unknown word based on context clues				
Add additional targets				

 Procedure and Data Collection: Run 10-20 trials per session with a **Y** or **N** per trial. Graph the overall percentage of the number correct on the Per Opportunity Graph.

Mastery Criterion: 80% correct across three consecutive sessions with two different instructors.

STUDENT: _____

RI.K.5   Identify the front cover, back cover, and title page of a book.

Materials: *Differentiated Instruction Cubes*, Classroom reading materials

Teaching Procedure: Prior to this activity, create cards for the *Differentiated Instruction Cubes* using the list of questions provided for RI.K.5 in Appendix C. While introducing a book to students, point to different parts of the book and ask them to identify what they are. For students who are struggling with this skill, you may need to start by having them point to a named part, and asking, "Show me the cover."

"What is this?" "Can you find the _____?" "What can you find on the _____?"

TARGET	INTRODUCED	MASTERED	GENERALIZATION PROBE	
Identifies the cover of a book				
Identifies the pages of a book				
Identifies the spine of a book				
Identifies the front cover of a book				
Identifies the back cover of a book				
Identifies the title page of a book				
Describes what information can be found on the front cover of a book				
Describes what information can be found on the back cover of a book				
Describes what information can be found on the spine of a book				
Describes what information can be found on the title page of a book				
Add additional targets				

Procedure and Data Collection: Run 10-20 trials per session with a **Y** or **N** per trial. Graph the overall percentage of the number correct on the Per Opportunity Graph.

Mastery Criterion: 80% correct across three consecutive sessions with two different instructors.

STUDENT: _____

RI.K.6

Name the author and illustrator of a text and define the role of each in presenting the ideas and information in a text.

Materials: *Differentiated Instruction Cubes, Reading Comprehension Cubes,* Informational text from classroom

Teaching Procedure: Prior to this activity, create cards for the *Differentiated Instruction Cubes* using the list of questions provided for RI.K.6 in Appendix C. Have multiple informational texts visible. Students take turns rolling the *Differentiated Instruction Cubes* and responding to the question for one of the reading materials. Questions about the author and illustrator are also included on the *Reading Comprehension Cubes* if you want to mix those questions in with other questions related to comprehension.

"Who wrote this story?" "What did the illustrator do for this story?"

TARGET	INTRODUCED	MASTERED	GENERALIZATION PROBE	
Identifies the author of an informational text				
Identifies the illustrator of an informational text				
Explains the role of an author in presenting the ideas and information in an informational text				
Explains the role of an illustrator in presenting the ideas and information in an informational text				
Add additional targets				

Procedure and Data Collection: Run 10-20 trials per session with a **Y** or **N** per trial. Graph the overall percentage of the number correct on the Per Opportunity Graph.

Mastery Criterion: 80% correct across three consecutive sessions with two different instructors.

STUDENT: _____

 RI.K.7   With prompting and support, describe the relationship between illustrations and the text in which they appear (e.g., what person, place, thing, or idea in the text an illustration depicts).

 Materials: *Differentiated Instruction Cubes*, Informational text from classroom

 Teaching Procedure: Prior to this activity, create cards for the *Differentiated Instruction Cubes* using the list of questions provided for RI.K.7 in Appendix C. Read an informational text with your students. After the story is complete, students take turns rolling the *Differentiated Instruction Cubes* and responding to the question for one of the reading materials.

 "Tell me about the picture." "What part of the story is this picture illustrating?" "Tell me what is happening in the story right now."

TARGET	INTRODUCED	MASTERED	GENERALIZATION PROBE	
Describes what is happening in the illustration prior to hearing/reading the text				
References the picture to retell what was read in the text				
Tells how the illustration relates to the text				
Add additional targets				

Procedure and Data Collection: Run 10-20 trials per session with a **Y** or **N** per trial. Graph the overall percentage of the number correct on the Per Opportunity Graph.

Mastery Criterion: 80% correct across three consecutive sessions with two different instructors.

STUDENT: _____

RI.K.8   With prompting and support, identify the reasons an author gives to support points in a text.

Materials: *Reading Comprehension Cubes*, *Differentiated Instruction Cubes*, Informational text from classroom

Teaching Procedure: Read an informational text with your students. Prior to reading, you can assign students specific questions with instructions to raise their hand when they hear the answer read aloud in the text. You can also provide individual copies of the text for students to underline or circle their responses. After reading is complete, students take turns rolling the *Reading Comprehension Cubes* and responding to the questions. The *Reading Comprehension Cubes* are a great tool for this standard, because if your students are at a skill level for which this standard is an appropriate target, the cubes allow for a mix of mastered skills with the target skill.

Sᴰ   "Why does the author believe this?" "What does the author say about _____?"

TARGET	INTRODUCED	MASTERED	GENERALIZATION PROBE
Responds to specific "why" questions related to how the author supports his/her points in the text			
Responds with one example of a supporting point when asked an open-ended question such as "How do you know the author thinks_____?"			
Responds with two-three examples of a supporting point when asked an open-ended question such as "How do you know the author thinks_____?"			
Add additional targets			

Procedure and Data Collection: Run 10-20 trials per session with a **Y** or **N** per trial. Graph the overall percentage of the number correct on the Per Opportunity Graph.

Mastery Criterion: 80% correct across three consecutive sessions with two different instructors.

STUDENT: _____

 RI.K.9 With prompting and support, identify basic similarities in and differences between two texts on the same topic (e.g., in illustrations, descriptions, or procedures).

 Materials: *Differentiated Instruction Cubes*, Two informational texts from the classroom on the same topic

 Teaching Procedure: Prior to this activity, create cards for the *Differentiated Instruction Cubes* using the list of questions provided for RI.K.9 in Appendix C. After reading the texts with the class, students take turns rolling the *Differentiated Instruction Cubes* and responding to the question about the reading materials. You can also split the class into two groups and assign one text to each group. When the students play with the cubes, a student from one group will respond to the question, and then a student from the other group will respond to the same question. After both responses, the class can discuss together the similarities and differences between the two responses.

 "What do they have in common?" "What idea do both stories talk about?"

TARGET	INTRODUCED	MASTERED	GENERALIZATION PROBE	
Responds accurately to questions about a specific detail such as "Does this story say the same thing about vehicles as the other story?"				
Responds accurately to questions about what two texts have in common				
Responds accurately to questions about how the information in two texts differs				
Add additional targets				

 Procedure and Data Collection: Run 10-20 trials per session with a **Y** or **N** per trial. Graph the overall percentage of the number correct on the Per Opportunity Graph.

Mastery Criterion: 80% correct across three consecutive sessions with two different instructors.

STUDENT: _____

RI.K.10   Actively engage in reading activities with purpose and understanding.

Materials: *Reading Comprehension Cubes, Differentiated Instruction Cubes, All Around Learning Circle Time Activity Set,* Informational texts or other reading materials from classroom

Teaching Procedure: Create a clear routine for starting group reading activities. This can include audio or visual cues that a transition is about to take place. Introduce group reading activity. Use visual and tactile materials such as puppets when applicable. After the story is complete, let students take turns rolling the *Reading Comprehension Cubes* and responding to questions to check for understanding. If your students cannot independently respond to questions from the *Reading Comprehension Cubes,* refer to the template in Appendix C to create customized cards to use with the *Differentiated Instruction Cubes.*

"What book do you want to read today?" Questions based on story being read during independent or group time.

TARGET	INTRODUCED	MASTERED	GENERALIZATION PROBE	
Chooses an appropriate book to read during independent time				
Attends to reading activities for 50% of the duration of the activity				
Responds to one question posed by the teacher during a reading activity				
Responds to three questions posed by the teacher during a reading activity				
Responds to five questions posed by the teacher during a reading activity				
Add additional targets				

Procedure and Data Collection: Run 10-20 trials per session with a **Y** or **N** per trial. Graph the overall percentage of the number correct on the Per Opportunity Graph.

Mastery Criterion: 80% correct across three consecutive sessions with two different instructors.

FOUNDATIONAL SKILLS OVERVIEW

· Understand how print is organized
· Identify words, syllables and sounds
· Decode words

CCSS CODE	STANDARD
RF.K.1	Demonstrate understanding of the organization and basic features of print.
RF.K.1.a	Follow words from left to right, top to bottom, and page by page.
RF.K.1.b	Recognize that spoken words are represented in written language by specific sequences of letters.
RF.K.1.c	Understand that words are separated by spaces in print.
RF.K.1.d	Recognize and name all upper- and lowercase letters of the alphabet.
RF.K.2	Demonstrate understanding of spoken words, syllables, and sounds (phonemes).
RF.K.2.a	Recognize and produce rhyming words.
RF.K.2.b	Count, pronounce, blend, and segment syllables in spoken words.
RF.K.2.c	Blend and segment onsets and rimes of single-syllable spoken words.
RF.K.2.d	Isolate and pronounce the initial, medial vowel, and final sounds (phonemes) in three-phoneme (consonant-vowel-consonant, or CVC) words. (This does not include CVCs ending with /l/, /r/, or /x/.)
RF.K.2.e	Add or substitute individual sounds in simple, one-syllable words to make new words.
RF.K.3	Know and apply grade-level phonics and word analysis skills in decoding words.
RF.K.3.a	Demonstrate basic knowledge of one-to-one letter-sound correspondences by producing the primary sound or many of the most frequent sounds for each consonant.
RF.K.3.b	Associate the long and short sounds with the common spellings (graphemes) for the five major vowels.
RF.K.3.c	Read common high-frequency words by sight (e.g., the, of, to, you, she, my, is, are, do, does).
RF.K.3.d	Distinguish between similarly spelled words by identifying the sounds of the letters that differ.
RF.K.4	Read emergent-reader texts with purpose and understanding.

KIT MATERIALS

- *Letters Pocket Chart Card Set*: RF.K.1.b, RF.K.1.d, RF.K.2.a, RF.K.2.c, RF.K.2.d, RF.K.2.e, RF.K.3.a, RF.K.3.b, RF.K.3.d
- *Differentiated Instruction Cubes*: RF.K.1.d, RF.K.2.a, RF.K.2.d, RF.K.2.e, RF.K.3.a, RF.K.3.b, RF.K.3.c, RF.K.4
- *Sight Words Pocket Chart Card Set*: RF.K.1.b, RF.K.2.a, RF.K.2.b, RF.K.3.c
- *Mid-Sized Pocket Chart*: RF.K.1.b, RF.K.1.d, RF.K.2.a, RF.K.2.b, RF.K.2.d, RF.K.2.e, RF.K.3.a, RF.K.3.b, RF.K.3.d
- *Writing and Art Kit*: RF.K.1.c
- *Chunk Stacker*: RF.K.1.b, RF.K.2.a, RF.K.2.c, RF.K.2.d, RF.K.3.c, RF.K.3.d
- *Reading Comprehension Cubes*: RF.K.4

CLASSROOM MATERIALS AND ACTIVITIES

- Classroom reading materials
- Text-rich environment (such as names on desks, word walls, common items labelled, etc.)
- Letter tiles from word games
- Cut-out letters: students use glue to put the letters together and form word families
- Index cards

TIP FOR GENERALIZATION

- A community walk can be a great activity for generalizing skills related to print concepts. Focus the walk on finding words in the neighborhood on signs, buildings, etc. Try to recognize the spaces between words and upper- and lowercase letters.
- A fantastic activity is a Sound Scavenger Hunt. Place a variety of letters around the room (print-outs, letter blocks, magnetic letters, etc.). Provide instructions such as "Find the letter that says 'ssss.' " You can also get students involved by allowing them to provide instructions too.

STUDENT: _____

RF.K.1*

Demonstrate understanding of the organization and basic features of print.

* This standard is divided into four more specified standards: RF.K.1.a, RF.K.1.b, RF.K.1.c, and RF.K.1.d. Once these four standards have been met, RF.K.1 is considered mastered.

RF.K.1.a

Follow words from left to right, top to bottom, and page by page.

Materials: Classroom reading materials

Teaching Procedure: Read a storybook with your students. Model the skills of following words from left to right and top to bottom. Point with your finger or use another visual cue as you read each word. Then allow students to practice the skill with the same book or another familiar book.

"Read with me." "Follow along."

TARGET	INTRODUCED	MASTERED	GENERALIZATION PROBE	
Follows words from left to right on the page				
Follows words from top to bottom on the page				
Turns just one page at a time				
Demonstrates knowledge of when to turn the page when reading familiar books				
Turns the page at the appropriate time in the reading				
Add additional targets				

Procedure and Data Collection: Run 10-20 trials per session with a **Y** or **N** per trial. Graph the overall percentage of the number correct on the Per Opportunity Graph.

Mastery Criterion: 80% correct across three consecutive sessions with two different instructors.

STUDENT: _____

RF.K.1*

Demonstrate understanding of the organization and basic features of print.

* This standard is divided into four more specified standards: RF.K.1.a, RF.K.1.b, RF.K.1.c, and RF.K.1.d. Once these four standards have been met, RF.K.1 is considered mastered.

RF.K.1.b

Recognize that spoken words are represented in written language by specific sequences of letters.

Materials: *Letters Pocket Chart Card Set*, *Sight Words Pocket Chart Card Set*, *Mid-Sized Pocket Chart*, *Chunk Stacker*

Teaching Procedure: Spell out words using the letter cards from the *Letters Pocket Chart Card Set*. Have students point to the letter that makes a specified sound. For example, if you have spelled the word C-A-T, you would ask, "What letter makes the _____ sound?" The student would then point to or pick up the correct letter. If students are not yet able to isolate sounds within a word, you can use the letter cards to ask what sounds individual letters make.

"What does _____ start with?" "What letter do you hear?"

TARGET	INTRODUCED	MASTERED	GENERALIZATION PROBE	
Identifies the letter that makes the initial sound in at least 25 CVC words				
Identifies the letter that makes the ending sound in at least 25 CVC words				
Identifies the letter that makes the middle sound in at least 25 CVC words				
Spells at least 25 CVC words phonetically upon hearing them spoken				
Spells novel CVC words phonetically upon hearing them spoken				
Add additional targets				

Procedure and Data Collection: Run 10-20 trials per session with a **Y** or **N** per trial. Graph the overall percentage of the number correct on the Per Opportunity Graph.

Mastery Criterion: 80% correct across three consecutive sessions with two different instructors.

STUDENT: _____

RF.K.1*   Demonstrate understanding of the organization and basic features of print.

* This standard is divided into four more specified standards: RF.K.1.a, RF.K.1.b, RF.K.1.c, and RF.K.1.d. Once these four standards have been met, RF.K.1 is considered mastered.

RF.K.1.c   Understand that words are separated by spaces in print.

 Materials: *Writing and Art Kit*, Popsicle sticks (optional)

 Teaching Procedure: After students have drawn pictures, ask them to write about their drawings. As students are writing, prompt them to put spaces between words. You can prompt them verbally, teach them to put a finger between words, or have them use a popsicle stick to indicate spaces between words.

 "Show me the word." "Can you read this?" "Write a sentence."

TARGET	INTRODUCED	MASTERED	GENERALIZATION PROBE	
Imitates pointing at individual words while reading				
Points to words in the environment while reading (such as first and last name written on the desk)				
Attempts to put appropriate spaces between words while writing				
Add additional targets				

Procedure and Data Collection: Run 10-20 trials per session with a **Y** or **N** per trial. Graph the overall percentage of the number correct on the Per Opportunity Graph.

Mastery Criterion: 80% correct across three consecutive sessions with two different instructors.

STUDENT: _____

 RF.K.1* Demonstrate understanding of the organization and basic features of print.

* This standard is divided into four more specified standards: RF.K.1.a, RF.K.1.b, RF.K.1.c, and RF.K.1.d. Once these four standards have been met, RF.K.1 is considered mastered.

RF.K.1.d Recognize and name all upper- and lowercase letters of the alphabet.

 Materials: *Letters Pocket Chart Card Set*, *Differentiated Instruction Cubes*, *Mid-Sized Pocket Chart*

 Teaching Procedure: Present the student with a card from the *Letters Pocket Chart Card Set* and ask, "What letter is this?" If the student is not yet able to respond to that question, you should put the target letter in a field of other letter cards and ask them to point to a specified letter. For example, you would place three letter cards on the table and ask the student to identify the letter "B." For students who have mastered many letters, you can use the *Differentiated Instruction Cubes* to roll different letters. Place a different card from the *Letters Pocket Chart Card Set* on each side of the cube and ask the student to identify the name of the letter showing on the face after rolling the cube.

 S^D "What letter is this?" "Name this letter." Presentation of written or printed letter.

TARGET	INTRODUCED	MASTERED	GENERALIZATION PROBE	
Recognizes and names the letters in his/her own name				
Recognizes and names 10 or more uppercase letters				
Recognizes and names all uppercase letters				
Recognizes and names 10 or more lowercase letters				
Recognizes and names all lowercase letters				
Add additional targets				

Procedure and Data Collection: Run 10-20 trials per session with a **Y** or **N** per trial. Graph the overall percentage of the number correct on the Per Opportunity Graph.

Mastery Criterion: 80% correct across three consecutive sessions with two different instructors.

Reading / Foundational Skills
Phonological Awareness
**RF.K.2: RF.K.2.a, RF.K.2.b,
RF.K.2.c, RF.K.2.d, RF.K.2.e**

STUDENT: _____

RF.K.2*   Demonstrate understanding of spoken words, syllables, and sounds (phonemes).

* This standard is divided into five more specified standards: RF.K.2.a, RF.K.2.b, RF.K.2.c, RF.K.2.d, and RF.K.2.e. Once these five standards have been met, RF.K.2 is considered mastered.

RF.K.2.a   Recognize and produce rhyming words.

Materials: *Chunk Stacker, Differentiated Instruction Cubes, Letters Pocket Chart Card Set, Sight Words Pocket Chart Card Set, Mid-Sized Pocket Chart*

Teaching Procedure: Select pink tiles from the *Chunk Stacker* game that you are going to target with your students. Give each student a stacker and one pink tile. Then give students blue tiles to place in front of the pink tiles in order to create rhyming words. For students who are doing well with rhyming or are highly motivated by rhyming, you can play the game as described in the instructions included with the *Chunk Stacker*. For students who may struggle with gripping the tiles from the game or playing it appropriately, you can also create words using the *Letters* cards in the *Differentiated Instruction Cubes*.

"What rhymes with _____?" "Tell me a word that rhymes with _____."

TARGET	INTRODUCED	MASTERED	GENERALIZATION PROBE	
Plays simple rhyming games and contributes three known rhymes				
Plays simple rhyming games and contributes five or more known rhymes				
Generates rhymes for any provided word				
Add additional targets				

Procedure and Data Collection: Run 10-20 trials per session with a **Y** or **N** per trial. Graph the overall percentage of the number correct on the Per Opportunity Graph.

Mastery Criterion: 80% correct across three consecutive sessions with two different instructors.

Reading/Foundational Skills
Phonological Awareness
RF.K.2: RF.K.2.a, RF.K.2.b,
RF.K.2.c, RF.K.2.d, RF.K.2.e

STUDENT: _____

RF.K.2*

Demonstrate understanding of spoken words, syllables, and sounds (phonemes).

* This standard is divided into five more specified standards: RF.K.2.a, RF.K.2.b, RF.K.2.c, RF.K.2.d, and RF.K.2.e. Once these five standards have been met, RF.K.2 is considered mastered.

RF.K.2.b

Count, pronounce, blend, and segment syllables in spoken words.

Materials: *Sight Words Pocket Chart Card Set, Mid-Sized Pocket Chart,* Index Cards (not included in kit)

Teaching Procedure: Prior to starting the lesson, ensure that students have space to move around and do not have access to other materials. Model for students how to break a word into syllables by clapping out each syllable. You can use index cards to break a word into parts, or even put a word on a sentence strip and have students cut the strip to separate the syllables. Movement is great with this activity, especially if you can add in movements such as, "Stomp for each syllable."

"Clap for each syllable." "How many syllables do you hear?"

TARGET	INTRODUCED	MASTERED	GENERALIZATION PROBE	
Claps out syllables in a word				
Counts syllables in a spoken word				
Repeats a spoken word and verbally segments the word by syllable				
Add additional targets				

Procedure and Data Collection: Run 10-20 trials per session with a **Y** or **N** per trial. Graph the overall percentage of the number correct on the Per Opportunity Graph.

Mastery Criterion: 80% correct across three consecutive sessions with two different instructors.

Reading/Foundational Skills
Phonological Awareness
**RF.K.2: RF.K.2.a, RF.K.2.b,
RF.K.2.c, RF.K.2.d, RF.K.2.e**

STUDENT: _____

RF.K.2*

Demonstrate understanding of spoken words, syllables, and sounds (phonemes).

* This standard is divided into five more specified standards: RF.K.2.a, RF.K.2.b, RF.K.2.c, RF.K.2.d, and RF.K.2.e. Once these five standards have been met, RF.K.2 is considered mastered.

RF.K.2.c

Blend and segment onsets and rimes of single-syllable spoken words.

 Materials: *Letters Pocket Chart Card Set, Chunk Stacker*

 Teaching Procedure: Start the lesson with whole group instruction using the letter cards from the *Letters Pocket Chart Card Set* to demonstrate the use of rime and onset. Then give each student a *Chunk Stacker*, several blue tiles and several pink tiles. Let students explore creating and sounding out new words. Help students identify if the word they've created is a real word or a nonsense word.

 "What does this say?" "Can you say that word?" "Is that a real word or a nonsense word?"

TARGET	INTRODUCED	MASTERED	GENERALIZATION PROBE	
Blends onset and rime to pronounce at least five words correctly				
Blends onset and rime to pronounce at least 10 words correctly				
Blends onset and rime to pronounce at least 25 words correctly				
Determines if a word is "real" or "nonsense" for five words				
Determines if a word is "real" or "nonsense" for 10 words				
Determines if a word is "real" or "nonsense" for 25 words				
Determines if a word is "real" or "nonsense" for novel words				
Add additional targets				

 Procedure and Data Collection: Run 10-20 trials per session with a **Y** or **N** per trial. Graph the overall percentage of the number correct on the Per Opportunity Graph.

Mastery Criterion: 80% correct across three consecutive sessions with two different instructors.

Reading/Foundational Skills
Phonological Awareness
**RF.K.2: RF.K.2.a, RF.K.2.b,
RF.K.2.c, RF.K.2.d, RF.K.2.e**

STUDENT: _____

RF.K.2*

Demonstrate understanding of spoken words, syllables, and sounds (phonemes).

* This standard is divided into five more specified standards: RF.K.2.a, RF.K.2.b, RF.K.2.c, RF.K.2.d, and RF.K.2.e. Once these five standards have been met, RF.K.2 is considered mastered.

RF.K.2.d

Isolate and pronounce the initial, medial vowel, and final sounds (phonemes) in three-phoneme (consonant-vowel-consonant, or CVC) words.* (This does not include CVCs ending with /l/, /r/, or /x/.)

*Words, syllables, or phonemes written in /slashes/ refer to their pronunciation or phonology. Thus, /CVC/ is a word with three phonemes regardless of the number of letters in the spelling of the word.

Materials: *Letters Pocket Chart Card Set, Mid-Sized Pocket Chart, Chunk Stacker, Differentiated Instruction Cubes*

Teaching Procedure: Use the cards from the *Letters Pocket Chart Card Set* to create CVC words on the table in front of students. Have students isolate and pronounce each sound. Physically move the letters closer together as a visual illustration of blending the sounds smoothly to read one word.

"What does this say?" "Can you pronounce this?" "Read this word."

TARGET	INTRODUCED	MASTERED	GENERALIZATION PROBE	
Isolates and pronounces each sound in CVC word correctly				
Blends sounds to smoothly read word for 10 known words				
Blends sounds to smoothly read word for 25 or more known words				
Blends sounds to read word for five or more novel words				
Add additional targets				

Procedure and Data Collection: Run 10-20 trials per session with a **Y** or **N** per trial. Graph the overall percentage of the number correct on the Per Opportunity Graph.

Mastery Criterion: 80% correct across three consecutive sessions with two different instructors.

Reading / Foundational Skills
Phonological Awareness
**RF.K.2: RF.K.2.a, RF.K.2.b,
RF.K.2.c, RF.K.2.d, RF.K.2.e**

STUDENT: _____

RF.K.2*

Demonstrate understanding of spoken words, syllables, and sounds (phonemes).

* This standard is divided into five more specified standards: RF.K.2.a, RF.K.2.b, RF.K.2.c, RF.K.2.d, and RF.K.2.e. Once these five standards have been met, RF.K.2 is considered mastered.

RF.K.2.e

Add or substitute individual sounds in simple, one-syllable words to make new words.

Materials: *Letters Pocket Chart Card Set, Mid-Sized Pocket Chart, Differentiated Instruction Cubes*

Teaching Procedure: Use the letter cards from the *Letters Pocket Chart Card Set* to create CVC words on the table in front of students. After asking students to sound out the word you have spelled on the table, replace one letter with a different letter and ask the students what the new word is. After modeling for them, have them create new words using the letter cards in the same manner.

"Can you change one letter to make a new word?" "What happens if I take away the _____ and replace it with a _____?"

TARGET	INTRODUCED	MASTERED	GENERALIZATION PROBE	
Adds or substitutes sounds in CVC words to make new words when prompted				
Adds or substitutes sounds in CVC words to make new words when prompted, and then accurately reads the new word				
Creates a new word by adding or substituting sound based on teacher instruction (For example, the word is "bat." The teacher instructs students to change it to "cat," and the student replaces the 'b' with a 'c'.)				
Add additional targets				

Procedure and Data Collection: Run 10-20 trials per session with a **Y** or **N** per trial. Graph the overall percentage of the number correct on the Per Opportunity Graph.

Mastery Criterion: 80% correct across three consecutive sessions with two different instructors.

STUDENT: _____

RF.K.3* Know and apply grade-level phonics and word analysis skills in decoding words.

> ** This standard is divided into four more specified standards: RF.K.3.a, RF.K.3.b, RF.K.3.c, and RF.K.3.d. Once these four standards have been met, RF.K.3 is considered mastered.*

RF.K.3.a Demonstrate basic knowledge of one-to-one letter-sound correspondences by producing the primary sound or many of the most frequent sounds for each consonant.

 Materials: *Letters Pocket Chart Card Set, Differentiated Instruction Cubes, Mid-Sized Pocket Chart*

 Teaching Procedure: Present a letter card from the *Letters Pocket Chart Card Set*. Ask the student what sound it makes. You can also write or print letters to place in the pockets of the *Differentiated Instruction Cubes*. Have students roll the cubes, and then name the letter facing up.

 "What sound does _____ make?" "What does _____ say?"

TARGET	INTRODUCED	MASTERED	GENERALIZATION PROBE	
Points to a letter upon hearing its sound in an array of three				
Points to a letter upon hearing its sound in a messy array of five or more				
Recognizes and names the letter-sound for 10 or more letters				
Recognizes and names the letter-sound for all letters				
Add additional targets				

Procedure and Data Collection: Run 10-20 trials per session with a **Y** or **N** per trial. Graph the overall percentage of the number correct on the Per Opportunity Graph.

Mastery Criterion: 80% correct across three consecutive sessions with two different instructors.

STUDENT: _____

RF.K.3* Know and apply grade-level phonics and word analysis skills in decoding words.

* This standard is divided into four more specified standards: RF.K.3.a, RF.K.3.b, RF.K.3.c, and RF.K.3.d. Once these four standards have been met, RF.K.3 is considered mastered.

RF.K.3.b Associate the long and short sounds with the common spellings (graphemes) for the five major vowels.

Materials: *Differentiated Instruction Cubes, Letters Pocket Chart Card Set, Mid-Sized Pocket Chart*

Teaching Procedure: For students who are just learning vowel sounds, you can use the *Differentiated Instruction Cubes*. On one cube, place a vowel on each side. On a second cube, write out "long," "short," along with the symbols for long and short and place them in the pockets of the cube. Students roll both cubes and pronounce the vowel as directed by the cubes. For students who have mastered the first two targets listed below, you can introduce more complex rules related to vowels. Use the letter cards from the *Letters Pocket Chart Card Set* to create CVC words, then make changes to illustrate how vowels change according to different rules. For example, spell out "bit." The students pronounce the word. Then add an "e" to make "bite" and have students pronounce the new word. Provide several examples, then allow students to create words on their own.

"What sound does _____ make?" "What does _____ say?"

TARGET	INTRODUCED	MASTERED	GENERALIZATION PROBE	
Recognizes and names the long sounds for all five vowels				
Recognizes and names the short sounds for all five vowels				
Recognizes the rule that if there is one vowel in a word, it is short				
Recognizes the rule that if there is an "e" at the end of a word, the vowel is long				
Recognizes the rule that if there are two vowels in a word, the first vowel is long and the second is silent				
Add additional targets				

Procedure and Data Collection: Run 10-20 trials per session with a **Y** or **N** per trial. Graph the overall percentage of the number correct on the Per Opportunity Graph.

Mastery Criterion: 80% correct across three consecutive sessions with two different instructors.

RF.K.3[*] Know and apply grade-level phonics and word analysis skills in decoding words.

* This standard is divided into four more specified standards: RF.K.3.a, RF.K.3.b, RF.K.3.c, and RF.K.3.d. Once these four standards have been met, RF.K.3 is considered mastered.

RF.K.3.c Read common high-frequency words by sight (e.g., the, of, to, you, she, my, is, are, do, does).

Materials: *Sight Words Pocket Chart Card Set, Differentiated Instruction Cubes, Chunk Stacker*

Teaching Procedure: Introduce a new sight word card. Pronounce the word for the students, and then use it in a sentence. Then place several sight word cards within view. Pronounce one of the sight words and have students find the word in the field of cards presented. *Note: It is important to teach sight words along with phonics so that students can use their knowledge of sight words to help them acquire and maintain decoding skills.*

"What does it say?" "Read this word." Presentation of word or word-card.

TARGET	INTRODUCED	MASTERED	GENERALIZATION PROBE	
Independently reads 10 or more sight words				
Independently reads 25 or more sight words				
Independently reads 100 or more sight words				
Add additional targets				

Procedure and Data Collection: Run 10-20 trials per session with a **Y** or **N** per trial. Graph the overall percentage of the number correct on the Per Opportunity Graph.

Mastery Criterion: 80% correct across three consecutive sessions with two different instructors.

STUDENT: _____

RF.K.3* Know and apply grade-level phonics and word analysis skills in decoding words.

* This standard is divided into four more specified standards: RF.K.3.a, RF.K.3.b, RF.K.3.c, and RF.K.3.d. Once these four standards have been met, RF.K.3 is considered mastered.

RF.K.3.d Distinguish between similarly spelled words by identifying the sounds of the letters that differ.

 Materials: *Chunk Stacker*, *Letters Pocket Chart Card Set*, *Mid-Sized Pocket Chart*, Index Cards (not included in kit)

 Teaching Procedure: When introducing this lesson, you should present index cards with two similar CVC words written. For example, one card would read "cat" and the other would read "cot." Ask students to identify which card says "cat." Do this for multiple pairs of words, prompting as necessary. As a follow up activity, provide each student with a *Chunk Stacker*, several blue tiles, and several pink tiles. Challenge students to create pairs of words, then record them.

 "What is different about these two words?" "Point to the letter that is different."

TARGET	INTRODUCED	MASTERED	GENERALIZATION PROBE	
Identifies the difference between 10 pairs of similar CVC words, such as "cat" and "cot" or "boy" and "toy"				
Identifies the difference between 25 pairs of similar CVC words				
Identifies the difference between 50 novel pairs of similar CVC words				
Add additional targets				

 Procedure and Data Collection: Run 10-20 trials per session with a **Y** or **N** per trial. Graph the overall percentage of the number correct on the Per Opportunity Graph.

Mastery Criterion: 80% correct across three consecutive sessions with two different instructors.

STUDENT: _____

RF.K.4 Read emergent-reader texts with purpose and understanding.

Materials: *Reading Comprehension Cubes, Differentiated Instruction Cubes,* Classroom reading materials

Teaching Procedure: Create a clear routine for starting independent reading activities. This can include audio or visual cues that a transition is about to take place. Make sure that your students understand how to choose appropriately leveled books. After each student is done reading, let students take turns rolling the *Reading Comprehension Cubes* and responding to questions to check for understanding. If your students cannot independently respond to questions from the *Reading Comprehension Cubes*, refer to the template in Appendix C to create customized cards to use with the *Differentiated Instruction Cubes*.

"Time to read." "Go choose a book." "What did you read about?"

TARGET	INTRODUCED	MASTERED	GENERALIZATION PROBE	
Reads an appropriate-level text out loud to teacher for three different texts				
Reads an appropriate-level text out loud to teacher when provided with a novel text				
Responds to questions checking for understanding with 80% accuracy after reading aloud with the teacher				
Responds to questions checking for understanding with 80% accuracy after reading aloud from a novel text with the teacher				
Chooses a variety of appropriate-level texts to read during independent reading or breaks				
Responds to questions checking for understanding with 80% accuracy after reading independently				
Add additional targets				

Procedure and Data Collection: Run 10-20 trials per session with a **Y** or **N** per trial. Graph the overall percentage of the number correct on the Per Opportunity Graph.

Mastery Criterion: 80% correct across three consecutive sessions with two different instructors.

WRITING OVERVIEW

· Draw, dictate, and write to share information
· Utilize digital tools to organize and share information
· Participate in conversations with both peers and adults to share and improve writing

CCSS CODE	STANDARD
W.K.1	Use a combination of drawing, dictating, and writing to compose opinion pieces in which they tell a reader the topic or the name of the book they are writing about and state an opinion or preference about the topic or book (e.g., My favorite book is...).
W.K.2	Use a combination of drawing, dictating, and writing to compose informative/explanatory texts in which they name what they are writing about and supply some information about the topic.
W.K.3	Use a combination of drawing, dictating, and writing to narrate a single event or several loosely linked events, tell about the events in the order in which they occurred, and provide a reaction to what happened.
W.K.5	With guidance and support from adults, respond to questions and suggestions from peers and add details to strengthen writing as needed.
W.K.6	With guidance and support from adults, explore a variety of digital tools to produce and publish writing, including in collaboration with peers.
W.K.7	Participate in shared research and writing projects (e.g., explore a number of books by a favorite author and express opinions about them).
W.K.8	With guidance and support from adults, recall information from experiences or gather information from provided sources to answer a question.

Note: W.K.4 begins in grade 3, W.K.9 begins in grade 4, W.K.10 begins in grade 3.

KIT MATERIALS

· *Writing and Art Kit*: W.K.1, W.K.2, W.K.3
· *Differentiated Instruction Cubes*: W.K.5, W.K.7

CLASSROOM MATERIALS AND ACTIVITIES

· Handwriting paper
· Reading materials and books
· Classroom art supplies
· Tactile writing: forming letters, pictures, and words with fingers in shaving cream, sand, or water
· Computers, tablets, camera

TIP FOR GENERALIZATION

You can use the *What Comes Next? ConversaCards* included in the kit to have students write or dictate a narrative about what is happening in the picture. You can also use comic strips without the text or other sequencing materials in the classroom for the same type of generalization activity.

Writing
Text Types and Purposes
W.K.1, W.K.2, W.K.3

STUDENT: _____

W.K.1 Use a combination of drawing, dictating, and writing to compose opinion pieces in which they tell a reader the topic or the name of the book they are writing about and state an opinion or preference about the topic or book (e.g., My favorite book is...).

Materials: *Writing and Art Kit*, Storybook from the classroom

Teaching Procedure: After reading a story, provide materials for students to respond to a prompt such as "My favorite book is..." or "I felt ____ about the story when ____ happened." Students may require varying levels of support for this standard. For some, you may provide visual prompts with potential responses, such as pictures of five different books the student has shown a preference for, or pictures of different emotions.

"Draw a picture about the story." "Tell me about your picture." "What should we write?"

TARGET	INTRODUCED	MASTERED	GENERALIZATION PROBE	
Draws a picture referencing a book or topic they've read about				
Dictates the topic or title of the book to be added to a drawing about that topic or book				
Dictates one sentence stating an opinion or preference to be added to a drawing about that topic or book				
Dictates two to three sentences stating an opinion or preference to be added to a drawing about that topic or book				
Writes the topic or title of the book on a drawing about that topic or book				
Writes one sentence stating an opinion or preference on a drawing about that topic or book				
Add additional targets				

Procedure and Data Collection: Run 10-20 trials per session with a **Y** or **N** per trial. Graph the overall percentage of the number correct on the Per Opportunity Graph.

Mastery Criterion: 80% correct across three consecutive sessions with two different instructors.

ABA Curriculum for the Common Core | Kindergarten | ELA

STUDENT: _____

W.K.2

Use a combination of drawing, dictating, and writing to compose informative/explanatory texts in which they name what they are writing about and supply some information about the topic.

Materials: _Writing and Art Kit_

Teaching Procedure: After reading an informative text or engaging in an activity such as a field trip, have students draw, dictate or write about what they learned. Based on each student's skill level, you can require that they write the topic at the top or have them select a topic from a field of choices provided by the teacher to glue to the top of the story. For example, provide three written or pictured topics such as "The Park," "The Grocery Store," and "The Movies." Students may require varying levels of support for this standard. For some, you may need to provide visual prompts with potential responses.

"Draw a picture to show me what happened." "Can you write about _____?"

TARGET	INTRODUCED	MASTERED	GENERALIZATION PROBE	
Draws a picture to compose an informative/ explanatory text				
Dictates the topic to be added to a drawing composed as an informative/explanatory text				
Dictates one sentence naming the topic and supplies some information about the topic to be added to a drawing composed as an informative/explanatory text				
Dictates two to three sentences naming the topic and supplies some information about the topic to be added to a drawing composed as an informative/ explanatory text				
Writes the topic on a drawing composed as an informative/explanatory text				
Writes one sentence naming the topic and supplies some information about the topic on a drawing composed as an informative/explanatory text				
Writes the topic on a drawing composed to narrate a single event				
Writes one sentence on a drawing of a picture composed to narrate a single event				
Add additional targets				

Procedure and Data Collection: Run 10-20 trials per session with a **Y** or **N** per trial. Graph the overall percentage of the number correct on the Per Opportunity Graph.

Mastery Criterion: 80% correct across three consecutive sessions with two different instructors.

W.K.3

Use a combination of drawing, dictating, and writing to narrate a single event or several loosely linked events, tell about the events in the order in which they occurred, and provide a reaction to what happened.

Materials: *Writing and Art Kit*

Teaching Procedure: After reading an informative text or engaging in an activity such as a cooking lesson or community walk, have students draw, dictate, or write about what they learned. Students may require varying levels of support for this standard, which may include textual or visual prompts. If students have not yet met the prerequisite skills for this standard, you may want to start with having them sequence events or information. For example, take pictures of the steps in a cooking lesson, and then have students place them in the correct order. Then, you can have students use those pictures to dictate or write about the information.

"Draw a picture to show me what happened." "Can you write about _____?"

TARGET	INTRODUCED	MASTERED	GENERALIZATION PROBE	
Draws a picture to narrate a single event				
Draws a picture to narrate a single event with the events placed in the order in which they occurred				
Draws a picture to narrate a single event with the events placed in the order in which they occurred, providing a reaction for what happened				
Dictates the topic to be added to a drawing of a picture composed to narrate a single event				
Dictates one sentence to be added to a drawing of a picture composed to narrate a single event				
Dictates two to three sentences to be added to a drawing of a picture telling the events in the order in which they occurred and providing a reaction to what happened				
Writes the topic on a drawing composed to narrate a single event				
Writes one sentence on a drawing of a picture composed to narrate a single event				
Add additional targets				

Procedure and Data Collection: Run 10-20 trials per session with a **Y** or **N** per trial. Graph the overall percentage of the number correct on the Per Opportunity Graph.

Mastery Criterion: 80% correct across three consecutive sessions with two different instructors.

STUDENT: _____

 W.K.5
With guidance and support from adults, respond to questions and suggestions from peers and add details to strengthen writing as needed.

 Materials: *Differentiated Instruction Cubes*

 Teaching Procedure: Prior to this activity, create cards for the *Differentiated Instruction Cubes* using the list of questions provided for W.K.5 in Appendix C. Share one student's written piece with the whole group. Have each student roll the *Differentiated Instruction Cubes* and respond to the prompt. You may also want to create customized cards specific to the current skill level of each student which you will also find in Appendix C.

 "Listen to the question." "Can you ask a peer for feedback?"

TARGET	INTRODUCED	MASTERED	GENERALIZATION PROBE	
Responds to questions from the teacher about a drawn/dictated/written piece				
Responds to one question from one peer about a drawn/dictated/written piece				
Responds to three questions from one peer about a drawn/dictated/written piece				
Responds to three questions from two or more peers about a drawn/dictated/written piece				
Listens to a suggestion from the teacher for a drawn/dictated/written piece and makes one change or addition to strengthen the piece				
Listens to a suggestion from one peer for a drawn/dictated/written piece and makes one change or addition to strengthen the piece				
Listens to a suggestion from two or more peers for a drawn/dictated/written piece and makes one change or addition to strengthen the piece				
Add additional targets				

 Procedure and Data Collection: Run 10-20 trials per session with a **Y** or **N** per trial. Graph the overall percentage of the number correct on the Per Opportunity Graph.

Mastery Criterion: 80% correct across three consecutive sessions with two different instructors.

STUDENT: _____

W.K.6 With guidance and support from adults, explore a variety of digital tools to produce and publish writing, including in collaboration with peers.

Materials: Computers, tablets, cameras (not included in kit)

Teaching Procedure: Introduce one digital tool at a time. When the student has mastered one digital tool, introduce another. For students with developmental delays, it is important to teach *functional* use of digital tools. Start with the tool you think your student is most likely to have success with and introduce a writing activity utilizing that tool (e.g., a fun app, Microsoft Word, etc.). Use textual or visual cues to help guide students through the appropriate steps to complete the task. For example, if you are requiring students to use a camera to take pictures and then write about a sequence of events, break it down into manageable, named steps that the student can reference.

S^D "Let's write." "Can you tell what happens next?" "What should we do next?"

TARGET	INTRODUCED	MASTERED	GENERALIZATION PROBE	
Uses computer or tablet program appropriately to complete a writing activity with 1:1 instruction from a teacher				
Uses computer or tablet program appropriately to complete a writing activity in group instruction				
Uses computer or tablet program appropriately and independently to complete a writing activity				
Shares computer or tablet program appropriately with one peer to complete an activity for at least one activity				
Shares computer or tablet program appropriately with one peer to complete an activity for at least three different activities				
Shares computer or tablet program appropriately with at least three peers to complete an activity for at least three different activities				
Add additional targets				

Procedure and Data Collection: Run 10-20 trials per session with a **Y** or **N** per trial. Graph the overall percentage of the number correct on the Per Opportunity Graph.

Mastery Criterion: 80% correct across three consecutive sessions with two different instructors.

STUDENT: _____

W.K.7 Participate in shared research and writing projects (e.g., explore a number of books by a favorite author and express opinions about them).

 Materials: *Differentiated Instruction Cubes,* Storybooks by the same author or about the same topic (not included in kit)

 Teaching Procedure: Prior to this activity, create cards for the *Differentiated Instruction Cubes* using the list of questions provided for W.K.7 in Appendix C. Read several books by the same author or on the same subject during whole group or independent reading. After students have read at least two books by the same author, have them take turns rolling the *Differentiated Instruction Cubes* and responding to the conversation prompts. You can also have each student pick one of the questions to write or draw about.

S^D "What's alike in all the stories?" "What did you learn in this book about ants that was not in the other book about ants?" "Do you have more questions after our research?"

TARGET	INTRODUCED	MASTERED	GENERALIZATION PROBE	
Reads two books by the same author or on the same subject and is able to describe similarities and differences with prompts and support				
Reads three or more books by the same author or on the same subject and is able to describe similarities and differences with prompts and support				
Reads three or more books by the same author or on the same subject and is able to describe opinions about the reading				
Illustrates opinions on research through drawing, writing, or using technology for at least one subject area or author				
Illustrates opinions on research through drawing, writing, or using technology for at least three different subject areas or authors				
Add additional targets				

 Procedure and Data Collection: Run 10-20 trials per session with a **Y** or **N** per trial. Graph the overall percentage of the number correct on the Per Opportunity Graph.

Mastery Criterion: 80% correct across three consecutive sessions with two different instructors.

W.K.8 With guidance and support from adults, recall information from experiences or gather information from provided sources to answer a question.

Materials: Visual, textual, or gestural prompts during conversation

Teaching Procedure: If students are prepared to start this standard,* utilize visual prompts when introducing the concept. You can use photos of field trips, recess, or classroom activities to have students practice providing information and answering questions. Over time, you should fade the picture prompts so that students are able to respond to questions without them.

If your student is not able to meet any of the prerequisite skills for this standard, you should assess using the VB-MAPP and start with developmentally appropriate goals.

"Can you find the answer in the text?" "Where can we find that information?" "Do you remember what we read about that last week?"

TARGET	INTRODUCED	MASTERED	GENERALIZATION PROBE
Finds information in a provided picture or image to respond to a question for at least three different pictures or images			
Finds information in a provided text to respond to a question for at least three different texts			
Recalls experience from within the last 30 minutes to respond to a question			
Recalls experience from within the last two hours to respond to a question			
Recalls experience from within the last day to respond to a question			
Recalls experience from within the last week to respond to a question			
Add additional targets			

Procedure and Data Collection: Run 10-20 trials per session with a **Y** or **N** per trial. Graph the overall percentage of the number correct on the Per Opportunity Graph.

Mastery Criterion: 80% correct across three consecutive sessions with two different instructors.

SPEAKING AND LISTENING OVERVIEW

- Participate in meaningful conversation about a variety of subjects
- Ask and answer questions
- Use language to provide details and express ideas clearly

CCSS CODE	STANDARD
SL.K.1	Participate in collaborative conversations with diverse partners about kindergarten topics and texts with peers and adults in small and larger groups.
SL.K.1.a	Follow agreed-upon rules for discussions (e.g., listening to others and taking turns speaking about the topics and texts under discussion).
SL.K.1.b	Continue a conversation through multiple exchanges.
SL.K.2	Confirm understanding of a text read aloud or information presented orally through other media by asking and answering questions about key details and requesting clarification if something is not understood.
SL.K.3	Ask and answer questions in order to seek help, get information, or clarify something that is not understood.
SL.K.4	Describe familiar people, places, things, and events, and, with prompting and support, provide additional detail.
SL.K.5	Add drawings or other visual displays to descriptions as desired to provide additional detail.
SL.K.6	Speak audibly and express thoughts, feelings, and ideas clearly.

KIT MATERIALS

- *ConversaCards (any set)*: SL.K.1.a, SL.K.1.b, SL.K.3
- *What Do You Like? ConversaCards*: SL.K.1.a, SL.K.6
- *What Do You Need? ConversaCards*: SL.K.6
- *Reading Comprehension Cubes*: SL.K.2
- *Writing and Art Kit*: SL.K.5
- *Differentiated Instruction Cubes*: SL.K.2

CLASSROOM MATERIALS AND ACTIVITIES

- Photos from newspapers or other publications
- Photos from field trips or other activities the class has engaged in

TIP FOR GENERALIZATION

A playful way to test for generalization is to bring out a student's favorite puppet or character doll and engage in conversation with them. You can speak as the character, have the student speak as the character, or both speak as characters.

Teaching language out of developmental order can be detrimental across all subject areas. While it holds true for all standards, in the strand for Speaking and Listening, it is even more crucial that you refer to individual student's assessment results to determine if these are appropriate learning goals at this point in their language development.

STUDENT: _____

SL.K.1* Participate in collaborative conversations with diverse partners about kindergarten topics and texts with peers and adults in small and larger groups.

> ** This standard is divided into two more specified standards: SL.K.1.a and SL.K.1.b.*
> *Once these two standards have been met, SL.K.1 is considered mastered.*

SL.K.1.a Follow agreed-upon rules for discussions (e.g., listening to others and taking turns speaking about the topics and texts under discussion).

Materials: *What Do You Like? ConversaCards, ConversaCards* (any set)

Teaching Procedure: Select one of the *ConversaCards* decks. (The *What Do You Like?* deck is an excellent choice for this standard, but any of them will work.) Place the card in view of all students participating in the conversation. Pose a question to start the conversation. You may want to include a visual cue of some sort, such as a talking stick, to help students take turns appropriately. After conversation is complete, you can select a new card to continue the activity. As students master the skill, you may want to introduce pictures from newspapers or other informational texts to practice conversation skills.

"Can you remind me about the rules before we start?" A gesture such as placing your fingers to your lips or holding out a palm to indicate to wait before speaking.

TARGET	INTRODUCED	MASTERED	GENERALIZATION PROBE	
Takes turns during conversation				
Attends to speaker for 80% of the time during a conversation				
Does not interrupt a speaker in 8 out of 10 trials				
Contributes on-topic statements to conversation in 8 out of 10 trials				
Add additional targets				

Procedure and Data Collection: Run 10-20 trials per session with a **Y** or **N** per trial. Graph the overall percentage of the number correct on the Per Opportunity Graph.

Mastery Criterion: 80% correct across three consecutive sessions with two different instructors.

STUDENT: _____

SL.K.1*

Participate in collaborative conversations with diverse partners about kindergarten topics and texts with peers and adults in small and larger groups.

* This standard is divided into two more specified standards: SL.K.1.a and SL.K.1.b. Once these two standards have been met, SL.K.1 is considered mastered.

SL.K.1.b

Continue a conversation through multiple exchanges.

Materials: *ConversaCards* (any set)

Teaching Procedure: Sit two students together. Introduce one of the *ConversaCards* so that both students can clearly see it. Then model an appropriate conversation with another adult or student. If you are using some type of visual cue for turn-taking (such as an arrow pointing to the current speaker or a talking stick), make sure you include it in your model. Then present the next card and have the students practice taking turns in conversation. If students are struggling with using the cards correctly, you may want to start with pictures you've taken on field trips/activities or with materials related to highly-motivating stories/characters.

Hearing name. "What do you think about it?" "Did you like the movie?" A statement addressed to the student.

TARGET	INTRODUCED	MASTERED	GENERALIZATION PROBE	
Responds to name by looking				
Responds to a question from the teacher				
Responds to a question from one peer				
Responds to a question from two to three different peers				
Engages in a conversation for two exchanges with a teacher				
Engages in a conversation for two exchanges with a peer				
Engages in a conversation for four to five exchanges with a teacher				
Engages in a conversation for four to five exchanges with a peer				
Engages in a conversation for four to five exchanges with a small group				
Add additional target				

Procedure and Data Collection: Run 10-20 trials per session with a **Y** or **N** per trial. Graph the overall percentage of the number correct on the Per Opportunity Graph.

Mastery Criterion: 80% correct across three consecutive sessions with two different instructors.

SL.K.2

Confirm understanding of a text read aloud or information presented orally through other media by asking and answering questions about key details and requesting clarification if something is not understood.

Materials: *Reading Comprehension Cubes, Differentiated Instruction Cubes,* Classroom reading materials

Teaching Procedure: After sharing a text, have students take turns rolling the *Reading Comprehension Cubes* and responding to questions. If students are struggling with those questions, you may need to create your own questions and use them with the *Differentiated Instruction Cubes.* Refer to the list of *Examples of Leading Statements* in Appendix B. You can copy the relevant questions and use the template in Appendix C to create customized cards to use for this standard.

"What happened in the story?" "Do you have any questions?" "Tell me more."

TARGET	INTRODUCED	MASTERED	GENERALIZATION PROBE	
Responds to "who," "what," and "where" questions about a text that has been read aloud for at least three different texts				
Responds to "when" questions about a text that has been read aloud for at least three different texts				
Responds to "why" questions about a text that has been read aloud for at least three different texts				
Responds to a random rotation of "wh" questions about a text that has been read aloud for a novel text				
Asks "wh" questions to access more information for at least three different types of "wh" questions				
Add additional targets				

Procedure and Data Collection: Run 10-20 trials per session with a **Y** or **N** per trial. Graph the overall percentage of the number correct on the Per Opportunity Graph.

Mastery Criterion: 80% correct across three consecutive sessions with two different instructors.

STUDENT: _____

SL.K.3

Ask and answer questions in order to seek help, get information, or clarify something that is not understood.

Materials: *ConversaCards* (any set)

Teaching Procedure: Present a novel card from the *ConversaCards*, or a novel image or activity. Provide students with textual prompts (such as an index card that says, "What..." as a prompt to ask a question beginning with "What") or leading questions. Refer to *Examples of Leading Statements* in Appendix B.

Presentation of unknown item or image. Providing a leading statement such as, "I did something really fun yesterday!"

TARGET	INTRODUCED	MASTERED	GENERALIZATION PROBE	
Asks for help when something is not understood				
Asks "what" questions to obtain more information from an adult				
Asks "what" questions to obtain more information from a peer				
Asks "who" and "where" questions to obtain more information from an adult				
Asks "who" and "where" questions to obtain more information from a peer				
Asks "wh" questions appropriately from both peers and adults to seek help, obtain information, or clarify				
Add additional targets				

Procedure and Data Collection: Run 10-20 trials per session with a **Y** or **N** per trial. Graph the overall percentage of the number correct on the Per Opportunity Graph.

Mastery Criterion: 80% correct across three consecutive sessions with two different instructors.

STUDENT: _____

SL.K.4 Describe familiar people, places, things, and events, and, with prompting and support, provide additional detail.

Materials: Visual, textual or gestural prompts during conversation

Teaching Procedure: Ask a student to describe something familiar, such as "Tell me about your dog." For some students, you may need to provide textual prompts that include sentence starters, such as "My dog is…" or, "One time, my dog…" Other students may require visual prompts in the form of pictures of the familiar person or item.

"Tell me about _____." "How would you describe _____?"

TARGET	INTRODUCED	MASTERED	GENERALIZATION PROBE	
Describes family				
Describes home				
Describes bedroom				
Describes favorite item				
Describes birthday party or other family event				
Describes recent outing, field trip, or school event				
Describes novel people, places, events, etc.				
Responds to questions to provide further detail about a description				
Add additional targets				

Procedure and Data Collection: Run 10-20 trials per session with a **Y** or **N** per trial. Graph the overall percentage of the number correct on the Per Opportunity Graph.

Mastery Criterion: 80% correct across three consecutive sessions with two different instructors.

STUDENT: _____

SL.K.5

Add drawings or other visual displays to descriptions as desired to provide additional detail.

Materials: *Writing and Art Kit*

Teaching Procedure: After the student has provided a verbal description of an item, person, or activity, ask them to show you what it looks like or draw a particular detail about their description. For many learners with developmental disabilities, it may be difficult to connect a drawing to a conversation, so prompts and redirection may be necessary.

"Can you show me what it looks like?" "Draw it."

TARGET	INTRODUCED	MASTERED	GENERALIZATION PROBE	
Draws family				
Draws home				
Draws bedroom				
Draws favorite item				
Draws birthday party or other family event				
Draws recent outing, field trip, or school event				
Draws novel people, places, events, etc.				
Responds to questions to provide further detail about a drawing				
Add additional targets				

Procedure and Data Collection: Run 10-20 trials per session with a **Y** or **N** per trial. Graph the overall percentage of the number correct on the Per Opportunity Graph.

Mastery Criterion: 80% correct across three consecutive sessions with two different instructors.

STUDENT: _____

SL.K.6

Speak audibly and express thoughts, feelings, and ideas clearly.

Materials: *What Do You Like? ConversaCards, What Do You Need? ConversaCards*

Teaching Procedure: Many students with developmental disabilities struggle with speaking audibly and clearly. It is important to provide motivating materials such as the *ConversaCards* or pictures of favorite characters to use for engaging in conversation. When starting this standard, you should select the cards from the *What Do You Like?* or *What Do You Need?* decks that you think will be most motivating to your students. It is also essential to use differential reinforcement to increase correct responding. For example, if you are working with a student who speaks too quietly, you would provide low-quality reinforcement for a quiet but correct response, and high-quality reinforcement for an audible and correct response. (Low and high quality reinforcers are determined by that individual's Preference Assessment results.) You may consider using tools such as an app that measures decibels so you can set a measureable goal.

"I can't hear you." "What did you say?" "How do you feel?"

TARGET	INTRODUCED	MASTERED	GENERALIZATION PROBE	
Speaks audibly				
Responds intelligibly to common questions (e.g., "What is your name?")				
Responds to questions in a complete sentence				
Responds to novel questions in a complete sentence				
Has a repertoire of two responses to "How do you feel?"				
Has a repertoire of four responses to "How do you feel?"				
Has a repertoire of five or more responses to "How do you feel?"				
Add additional targets				

Procedure and Data Collection: Run 10-20 trials per session with a **Y** or **N** per trial. Graph the overall percentage of the number correct on the Per Opportunity Graph.

Mastery Criterion: 80% correct across three consecutive sessions with two different instructors.

LANGUAGE OVERVIEW

- Use grammar appropriately when speaking and writing
- Understand conventions of English language
- Use context clues to determine meanings of new words

CCSS CODE	STANDARD
L.K.1	Demonstrate command of the conventions of standard English grammar and usage when writing or speaking.
L.K.1.a	Print many upper- and lowercase letters.
L.K.1.b	Use frequently occurring nouns and verbs.
L.K.1.c	Form regular plural nouns orally by adding /s/ or /es/ (e.g., dog, dogs; wish, wishes).
L.K.1.d	Understand and use question words (interrogatives) (e.g., who, what, where, when, why, how).
L.K.1.e	Use the most frequently occurring prepositions (e.g., to, from, in, out, on, off, for, of, by, with).
L.K.1.f	Produce and expand complete sentences in shared language activities.
L.K.2	Demonstrate command of the conventions of standard English capitalization, punctuation, and spelling when writing.
L.K.2.a	Capitalize the first word in a sentence and the pronoun.
L.K.2.b	Recognize and name end punctuation.
L.K.2.c	Write a letter or letters for most consonant and short-vowel sounds (phonemes).
L.K.2.d	Spell simple words phonetically, drawing on knowledge of sound-letter relationships.
L.K.4	Determine or clarify the meaning of unknown or multiple-meaning words and phrases based on kindergarten reading and content.
L.K.4.a	Identify new meanings for familiar words and apply them accurately (e.g., knowing duck is a bird and learning the verb to duck).
L.K.4.b	Use the most frequently occurring inflections and affixes (e.g., -ed, -s, re-, un-, pre-, -ful, -less) as a clue to the meaning of an unknown word.
L.K.5	With guidance and support from adults, explore word relationships and nuances in word meanings.
L.K.5.a	Sort common objects into categories (e.g., shapes, foods) to gain a sense of the concepts the categories represent.
L.K.5.b	Demonstrate understanding of frequently occurring verbs and adjectives by relating them to their opposites (antonyms).
L.K.5.c	Identify real-life connections between words and their use (e.g., note places at school that are colorful).
L.K.5.d	Distinguish shades of meaning among verbs describing the same general action (e.g., walk, march, strut, prance) by acting out the meanings.
L.K.6	Use words and phrases acquired through conversations, reading and being read to, and responding to texts.

Note: L.K.3 begins in grade 2.

KIT MATERIALS

- *Writing and Art Kit*: L.K.1.a, L.K.2.a, L.K.2.c, L.K.2.d
- *What Do You Do With It? ConversaCards*: L.K.1.b, L.K.5.c
- *What Happened? ConversaCards*: L.K.1.d
- *What Do You Need? ConversaCards*: L.K.1.d
- *I Can Do That! Game*: L.K.1.e, L.K.5.d
- *Following Auditory Directions*: L.K.1.e
- *Reading Comprehension Cubes*: L.K.4.a
- *Differentiated Instruction Cubes*: L.K.2.b, L.K.4.a, L.K.5.b, L.K.5.c, L.K.5.d
- *3D Feel and Find*: L.K.5.a
- *Mighty Mind* : L.K.5.a
- *All Around Learning Circle Time Activity Set*: L.K.5.a, L.K.6

CLASSROOM MATERIALS AND ACTIVITIES

- Classroom art supplies, handwriting paper
- Classroom reading materials
- Groups of 1-5 items to practice using singular and plural nouns
- Classroom or Playground Scavenger Hunt to practice using prepositions
- Community Word Hunt: On a community walk, students name objects, describe them, and label their categories.
- Act It Out: Use the list for L.K.5.b or L.K.5.d in Appendix C to create cards. A student or teacher picks a card and everyone acts it out.

TIPS FOR GENERALIZATION

- A modified version of Hide and Seek is useful for generalizing spoken English skills. Designate one student as the Speaker. All other students cover their eyes. The adult hides a pre-determined item, such as a toy car. The speaker then has to describe where the item is hidden using words; they should not physically indicate where their peers should look.
- Play a Simon Says game with upper- and lowercase letters. Some instructions will be to write a lowercase letter or uppercase letter, but they can be mixed in with other tasks that are fun for the students, such as motor tasks.
- Place large sheets of paper labeled with categories such as animals, vehicles and foods within reach of students. Each student cuts out pictures from magazines and/or newspapers, and then glues them on the appropriate category sheet.

Language
Conventions of Standard English
L.K.1: L.K.1.a, L.K.1.b, L.K.1.c, L.K.1.d, L.K.1.e, L.K.1.f
L.K.2: L.K.2.a, L.K.2.b, L.K.2.c, L.K.2.d

STUDENT: _____

L.K.1*

Demonstrate command of the conventions of standard English grammar and usage when writing or speaking.

* This standard is divided into six more specified standards: L.K.1.a, L.K.1.b, L.K.1.c, L.K.1.d, L.K.1.e, and L.K.1.f. Once these six standards have been met, L.K.1 is considered mastered.

L.K.1.a

Print many upper- and lowercase letters.

Materials: *Writing and Art Kit*

Teaching Procedure: Provide students with paper and writing utensils from the *Writing and Art Kit*. Model writing the letter you expect students to print. Allow them time to practice, and provide prompts as needed. For learners who find writing activities aversive, provide individualized, highly-motivating activities and materials such as different types of paper or the opportunity to create letters by tracing their finger in sand.

"Show me a _____." "Write a _____." "What does a _____ look like?"

TARGET	INTRODUCED	MASTERED	GENERALIZATION PROBE	
Traces at least five uppercase letters staying within one centimeter of the line				
Traces at least 10 uppercase letters staying within one centimeter of the line				
Traces all uppercase letters staying within one centimeter of the line				
Independently writes at least five uppercase letters				
Independently writes first name in all uppercase letters				
Independently writes at least 10 uppercase letters				
Independently writes all uppercase letters				
Traces at least five lowercase letters staying within one centimeter of the line				
Traces at least 10 lowercase letters staying within one centimeter of the line				
Traces all lowercase letters staying within one centimeter of the line				
Independently writes at least five lowercase letters				
Independently writes at least 10 lowercase letters				
Independently writes all lowercase letters				

Procedure and Data Collection: Run 10-20 trials per session with a **Y** or **N** per trial. Graph the overall percentage of the number correct on the Per Opportunity Graph.

Mastery Criterion: 80% correct across three consecutive sessions with two different instructors.

Language
Conventions of Standard English
L.K.1: L.K.1.a, L.K.1.b, L.K.1.c, L.K.1.d, L.K.1.e, L.K.1.f
L.K.2: L.K.2.a, L.K.2.b, L.K.2.c, L.K.2.d

STUDENT: _____

L.K.1* Demonstrate command of the conventions of standard English grammar and usage when writing or speaking.

* This standard is divided into six more specified standards: L.K.1.a, L.K.1.b, L.K.1.c, L.K.1.d, L.K.1.e, and L.K.1.f. Once these six standards have been met, L.K.1 is considered mastered.

L.K.1.b Use frequently occurring nouns and verbs.

Materials: *What Do You Do with It? ConversaCards*

Teaching Procedure: Show the students one card. Ask students what they see in the picture, or what the person is doing in the picture. Choose appropriate targets for each individual student based on their current skill level. For students who are struggling with identifying nouns and verbs with pictures, you may want to start with having them identify objects in the room or identify nouns and verbs in clips of their favorite TV shows.

** NOTE: If your student is not able to meet any of the prerequisite skills for this standard, you should assess using the VB-MAPP and start with developmentally appropriate goals. **

"What is she doing?" "Tell me what's happening." "What's happening in this picture?"

TARGET	INTRODUCED	MASTERED	GENERALIZATION PROBE	
Labels three exemplars of 100 different common items, including pictures and objects				
Labels three exemplars of 500 different common items, including pictures and objects				
Labels 25 different actions including pictures of actions and observed actions in the natural environment (For example, when asked, "What is Sally doing?" the student responds, "Walking.")				
Combines nouns and verbs to describe what is happening in a picture or in situ (For example, when asked, "What is the teacher doing?" the student responds, "Reading book.")				
Acquires new nouns and verbs in less than five trials				
Acquires new nouns and verbs from exposure in the natural environment				
Add additional targets				

Procedure and Data Collection: Run 10-20 trials per session with a **Y** or **N** per trial. Graph the overall percentage of the number correct on the Per Opportunity Graph.

Mastery Criterion: 80% correct across three consecutive sessions with two different instructors.

Language
Conventions of Standard English
L.K.1: L.K.1.a, L.K.1.b, L.K.1.c, L.K.1.d, L.K.1.e, L.K.1.f
L.K.2: L.K.2.a, L.K.2.b, L.K.2.c, L.K.2.d

STUDENT: _____

L.K.1*

Demonstrate command of the conventions of standard English grammar and usage when writing or speaking.

* This standard is divided into six more specified standards: L.K.1.a, L.K.1.b, L.K.1.c, L.K.1.d, L.K.1.e, and L.K.1.f. Once these six standards have been met, L.K.1 is considered mastered.

L.K.1.c

Form regular plural nouns orally by adding /s/ or /es/ (e.g., dog, dogs; wish, wishes).

Materials: Boxes, a variety of classroom or household items (not included in kit)

Teaching Procedure: Prepare several pairs of boxes. For each pair, one box will contain a single object, while the other box will have multiple objects. For example, one box will have one shell in it, while the other box will have three shells in it. Present a pair of boxes and model for students "One shell, three shells." Present additional pairs and have students demonstrate proper use of plural nouns. You can also have students make their own samples by collecting classroom objects, arts and crafts materials, or found items on a nature walk.

"Tell me about the picture." "What do you have?" "How many are there?"

TARGET	INTRODUCED	MASTERED	GENERALIZATION PROBE	
Adds /s/ or /es/ to plural words when speaking				
Uses singular words correctly when speaking; does not add /s/ or /es/ to singular words				
Adds /s/ or /es/ to plural words when writing				
Uses singular words correctly when writing; does not add /s/ or /es/ to singular words				
Add additional targets				

Procedure and Data Collection: Run 10-20 trials per session with a **Y** or **N** per trial.
Graph the overall percentage of the number correct on the Per Opportunity Graph.

Mastery Criterion: 80% correct across three consecutive sessions with two different instructors.

Language
Conventions of Standard English
L.K.1: L.K.1.a, L.K.1.b, L.K.1.c, L.K.1.d, L.K.1.e, L.K.1.f
L.K.2: L.K.2.a, L.K.2.b, L.K.2.c, L.K.2.d

STUDENT: _____

 L.K.1* Demonstrate command of the conventions of standard English grammar and usage when writing or speaking.

** This standard is divided into six more specified standards: L.K.1.a, L.K.1.b, L.K.1.c, L.K.1.d, L.K.1.e, and L.K.1.f.
Once these six standards have been met, L.K.1 is considered mastered.*

 L.K.1.d Understand and use question words (interrogatives) (e.g., who, what, where, when, why, how).

 Materials: *What Happened? ConversaCards, What Do You Need? Conversacards*

 Teaching Procedure: Prior to the lesson, select cards that will help students practice target interrogative words. Place the card in front of the students and ask a "wh" question about the picture. You can use the same card to ask students different types of questions, allowing for easy differentiation. Once students have mastered responding to each type of interrogative, you can introduce having them ask questions about a card to the teacher or to peers. You can do the same type of activity with pictures from newspapers, magazines, and informational texts, or with pictures from familiar books.

 S^D Presentation of unknown item or image. "Who is this?"

TARGET	INTRODUCED	MASTERED	GENERALIZATION PROBE	
Responds appropriately to a random rotation of "who," "what," and "where" questions related to a picture (Appropriately does not mean correctly, but means the student is responding to the correct question, instead of responding with a "who" answer to a "where" question.)				
Responds appropriately to "when" questions (For example, when the teacher asks, "When are we going to lunch?" the student can say, "After reading.")				
Responds appropriately to "why" questions				
Uses "who," "what," and "where" questions to get information				
Uses "why" as a single-word question				
Uses "why" in a full sentence to get more information				
Uses "when" questions to get information				
Add additional targets				

 Procedure and Data Collection: Run 10-20 trials per session with a **Y** or **N** per trial.
Graph the overall percentage of the number correct on the Per Opportunity Graph.

Mastery Criterion: 80% correct across three consecutive sessions with two different instructors.

Language
Conventions of Standard English
L.K.1: L.K.1.a, L.K.1.b, L.K.1.c, L.K.1.d, L.K.1.e, L.K.1.f
L.K.2: L.K.2.a, L.K.2.b, L.K.2.c, L.K.2.d

STUDENT: _____

L.K.1*

Demonstrate command of the conventions of standard English grammar and usage when writing or speaking.

* This standard is divided into six more specified standards: L.K.1.a, L.K.1.b, L.K.1.c, L.K.1.d, L.K.1.e, and L.K.1.f.
Once these six standards have been met, L.K.1 is considered mastered.

L.K.1.e

Use the most frequently occurring prepositions (e.g., to, from, in, out, on, off, for, of, by, with).

 Materials: *I Can Do That! Game, Following Auditory Directions*

 Teaching Procedure: Play *I Can Do That!* as a fun way to introduce and model prepositions. The game requires students to pick three cards that provide instructions using prepositions. You may want to modify the game to include fewer cards while still using the motivating materials to practice using prepositions.

 "Put the _____ in the _____." "Where is the _____?" "Can you find it? It's by the pencil."

TARGET	INTRODUCED	MASTERED	GENERALIZATION PROBE	
Uses "to" to respond to questions and provide information				
Uses "from" to respond to questions and provide information				
Uses "in" to respond to questions and provide information				
Uses "out" to respond to questions and provide information				
Uses "on" to respond to questions and provide information				
Uses "off" to respond to questions and provide information				
Uses "for" to respond to questions and provide information				
Uses "by" to respond to questions and provide information				
Uses "of" to respond to questions and provide information				
Uses "with" to respond to questions and provide information				
Add additional target				

 Procedure and Data Collection: Run 10-20 trials per session with a **Y** or **N** per trial. Graph the overall percentage of the number correct on the Per Opportunity Graph.

Mastery Criterion: 80% correct across three consecutive sessions with two different instructors.

Language
Conventions of Standard English
L.K.1: L.K.1.a, L.K.1.b, L.K.1.c, L.K.1.d, L.K.1.e, L.K.1.f
L.K.2: L.K.2.a, L.K.2.b, L.K.2.c, L.K.2.d   STUDENT: _____

L.K.1*

Demonstrate command of the conventions of standard English grammar and usage when writing or speaking.

* This standard is divided into six more specified standards: L.K.1.a, L.K.1.b, L.K.1.c, L.K.1.d, L.K.1.e, and L.K.1.f. Once these six standards have been met, L.K.1 is considered mastered.

L.K.1.f

Produce and expand complete sentences in shared language activities.

** NOTE: L.K.1.b should be mastered prior to introducing this program.**

Materials: Visual, textual, or gestural prompts during conversations

Teaching Procedure: During the circle time routine, ask the student a question about the current activity. You can point to specific items as a gestural prompt to help students respond. For example, you might point to a picture in a book and ask "What is the boy doing?" The appropriate response may be "boy jumping" or "the boy is jumping" depending on your student's current target skill. For each prerequisite step listed below, it is important for the student to use dozens of each combination before moving on to the next step. For example, you would not move on to the next step if the student is only emitting five noun-verb combinations.

"Tell me about _____." "Can you tell me more?"

TARGET	INTRODUCED	MASTERED	GENERALIZATION PROBE	
Responds to questions with a noun-verb combination				
Responds to questions with a sentence composed of a noun, verb, and adjective or adverb				
Uses complete sentences to request items				
Responds to conversation initiated by a teacher in a complete sentence				
Responds to conversation initiated by a peer in a complete sentence				
Engages in circle time, story time, or other language activities with reciprocal language				
Add additional targets				

Procedure and Data Collection: Run 10-20 trials per session with a **Y** or **N** per trial. Graph the overall percentage of the number correct on the Per Opportunity Graph.

Mastery Criterion: 80% correct across three consecutive sessions with two different instructors.

Language
Conventions of Standard English
L.K.1: L.K.1.a, L.K.1.b, L.K.1.c, L.K.1.d, L.K.1.e, L.K.1.f
L.K.2: L.K.2.a, L.K.2.b, L.K.2.c, L.K.2.d

L.K.2*

Demonstrate command of the conventions of standard English capitalization, punctuation, and spelling when writing.

* This standard is divided into four more specified standards: L.K.2.a, L.K.2.b, L.K.2.c, and L.K.2.d. Once these four standards have been met, L.K.2 is considered mastered.

L.K.2.a

Capitalize the first word in a sentence and the pronoun "I."

**NOTE: Prior to introducing this skill, your student must be able to identify and differentiate upper- and lowercase letters. This skill should be taught in conjunction with W.K.1, W.K.2, and W.K.3.**

Materials: _Writing and Art Kit_

Teaching Procedure: While students are writing about a drawing, a book they've read, or a recent event, prompt them to begin sentences with a capital letter. While teaching, model an error (such as writing the pronoun "I" in lower case) and ask students, "What's wrong?"

"Write this sentence: _____." "Can you write it down?" Presentation of sentence to be copied.

TARGET	INTRODUCED	MASTERED	GENERALIZATION PROBE	
Capitalizes the first word in a sentence when provided with a verbal reminder to correct an error				
Capitalizes the first word in a sentence when provided with a verbal reminder prior to the activity				
Capitalizes the pronoun "I" when provided with a verbal reminder to correct an error				
Independently capitalizes the pronoun "I"				
Independently capitalizes the first word in a sentence				
Add additional targets				

Procedure and Data Collection: Run 10-20 trials per session with a **Y** or **N** per trial. Graph the overall percentage of the number correct on the Per Opportunity Graph.

Mastery Criterion: 80% correct across three consecutive sessions with two different instructors.

Language
Conventions of Standard English
L.K.1: L.K.1.a, L.K.1.b, L.K.1.c, L.K.1.d, L.K.1.e, L.K.1.f
L.K.2: L.K.2.a, L.K.2.b, L.K.2.c, L.K.2.d

STUDENT: _____

 L.K.2* Demonstrate command of the conventions of standard English capitalization, punctuation, and spelling when writing.

* This standard is divided into four more specified standards: L.K.2.a, L.K.2.b, L.K.2.c, and L.K.2.d. Once these four standards have been met, L.K.2 is considered mastered.

L.K.2.b Recognize and name end punctuation.

 Materials: *Differentiated Instruction Cubes*

 Teaching Procedure: Prior to this activity, create cards for the *Differentiated Instruction Cubes* using the list of punctuation and statements provided for L.K.2.b in Appendix C. While reading a book, point out the target punctuation mark and explain why it is used there. After students have learned at least two punctuation marks, introduce the *Differentiated Instruction Cubes* activity. If students aren't yet able to independently name a punctuation mark, place three or more examples of punctuation marks on the table or floor and ask a student to find one, such as, "Can you show me the question mark?"

 "What is this?" "Tell me its name."

TARGET	INTRODUCED	MASTERED	GENERALIZATION PROBE	
Names a period when asked				
Names a question mark when asked				
Names an exclamation point when asked				
Add additional targets				

Procedure and Data Collection: Run 10-20 trials per session with a **Y** or **N** per trial. Graph the overall percentage of the number correct on the Per Opportunity Graph.

Mastery Criterion: 80% correct across three consecutive sessions with two different instructors.

Language
Conventions of Standard English
L.K.1: L.K.1.a, L.K.1.b, L.K.1.c, L.K.1.d, L.K.1.e, L.K.1.f
L.K.2: L.K.2.a, L.K.2.b, L.K.2.c, L.K.2.d

STUDENT: _____

L.K.2*

Demonstrate command of the conventions of standard English capitalization, punctuation, and spelling when writing.

** This standard is divided into four more specified standards: L.K.2.a, L.K.2.b, L.K.2.c, and L.K.2.d.
Once these four standards have been met, L.K.2 is considered mastered.*

L.K.2.c

Write a letter or letters for most consonant and short-vowel sounds (phonemes).

Materials: *Writing and Art Kit*

Teaching Procedure: Present paper and writing materials from the *Writing and Art Kit*. Tell students you are going to play the "Sound Game." Name a sound, and then have students write down the letter that makes that sound.

"Write the letter that says _____." "What letter makes a _____ sound?" "Can you show me _____?"

TARGET	INTRODUCED	MASTERED	GENERALIZATION PROBE	
Writes a letter for five or more consonant or short-vowel sounds				
Writes a letter for 10 or more consonant or short-vowel sounds				
Writes a letter for 20 or more consonant or short-vowel sounds				
Add additional targets				

Procedure and Data Collection: Run 10-20 trials per session with a **Y** or **N** per trial.
Graph the overall percentage of the number correct on the Per Opportunity Graph.

Mastery Criterion: 80% correct across three consecutive sessions with two different instructors.

Language
Conventions of Standard English
**L.K.1: L.K.1.a, L.K.1.b, L.K.1.c, L.K.1.d, L.K.1.e, L.K.1.f
L.K.2: L.K.2.a, L.K.2.b, L.K.2.c, L.K.2.d**

STUDENT: _____

L.K.2*

Demonstrate command of the conventions of standard English capitalization, punctuation, and spelling when writing.

** This standard is divided into four more specified standards: L.K.2.a, L.K.2.b, L.K.2.c, and L.K.2.d.
Once these four standards have been met, L.K.2 is considered mastered.*

L.K.2.d

Spell simple words phonetically, drawing on knowledge of sound-letter relationships.

NOTE: Prior to introducing this skill, your student must have mastered L.K.2.c.

Materials: *Writing and Art Kit*

Teaching Procedure: Present paper and writing materials from the *Writing and Art Kit*. Pronounce a word and ask your students to spell it on their papers. You may split up your class into groups of students with similar goals, such as having one group working on words that have the short 'a' sound, while another group works on a random rotation of words that have the short 'a'/short 'e'/short 'o' sounds.

"Write _____." "Can you spell _____?"

TARGET	INTRODUCED	MASTERED	GENERALIZATION PROBE	
Spells at least five CVC words phonetically				
Spells at least 20 CVC words phonetically				
Spells any simple word phonetically upon request				
Add additional targets				

Procedure and Data Collection: Run 10-20 trials per session with a **Y** or **N** per trial.
Graph the overall percentage of the number correct on the Per Opportunity Graph.

Mastery Criterion: 80% correct across three consecutive sessions with two different instructors.

Language
Vocabulary Acquisition and Use
L.K.4: L.K.4.a, L.K.4.b
L.K.5: L.K.5.a, L.K.5.b, L.K.5.c, L.K.5.d, L.K.6

STUDENT: _____

L.K.4* Determine or clarify the meaning of unknown or multiple-meaning words and phrases based on kindergarten reading and content.

* This standard is divided into two more specified standards: L.K.4.a and L.K.4.b. Once these two standards have been met, L.K.4 is considered mastered.

L.K.4.a Identify new meanings for familiar words and apply them accurately (e.g., knowing duck is a bird and learning the verb to duck).

NOTE: Prior to introducing this skill, student should have mastered L.K.1.b.

Materials: *Differentiated Instruction Cubes, Reading Comprehension Cubes*

Teaching Procedure: Prior to this activity, create cards for the *Differentiated Instruction Cubes* using the list of words provided for L.K.4.a in Appendix C. Introduce several pairs of words, and demonstrate their meanings by acting them out (such as acting out the noun "fly" and the verb to "fly") or by showing illustrations of their meanings. Then provide students with the *Differentiated Instruction Cubes*. Students can choose to use the word in two different sentences demonstrating understanding of each meaning, or to act out both meanings of the word.

"What do you think that means?" "Can you find a clue that might help us figure out the meaning of _____?"

TARGET	INTRODUCED	MASTERED	GENERALIZATION PROBE	
Understands new meanings for five or more familiar words and uses them correctly				
Understands new meanings for 10 or more familiar words and uses them correctly				
Add additional targets				

Procedure and Data Collection: Run 10-20 trials per session with a **Y** or **N** per trial. Graph the overall percentage of the number correct on the Per Opportunity Graph.

Mastery Criterion: 80% correct across three consecutive sessions with two different instructors.

Language
Vocabulary Acquisition and Use
L.K.4: L.K.4.a, L.K.4.b
L.K.5: L.K.5.a, L.K.5.b, L.K.5.c, L.K.5.d, L.K.6

STUDENT: _____

L.K.4* Determine or clarify the meaning of unknown or multiple-meaning words and phrases based on kindergarten reading and content.

** This standard is divided into two more specified standards: L.K.4.a and L.K.4.b.
Once these two standards have been met, L.K.4 is considered mastered.*

L.K.4.b Use the most frequently occurring inflections and affixes (e.g., -ed, -s, re-, un-, pre-, -ful, -less) as a clue to the meaning of an unknown word.

Materials: Visual, textual, or gestural prompts during conversation

Teaching Procedure: Focus a lesson on one inflection or affix. Provide multiple examples and non-examples. Then read or tell a story that uses the inflection or affix several times and ask students about its meaning in the context of the story.

"What's another word for that?" "Today he walks. Yesterday he _____." "What did you do yesterday?" "How many do you have?"

TARGET	INTRODUCED	MASTERED	GENERALIZATION PROBE	
Adds -ed to the end of a word to show that the action happened in the past				
Adds -s to the end of the word to show it is plural				
Adds un- to the beginning of a word to show the action is not completed				
Adds pre- to the beginning of a word to show that something was done prior to the action				
Adds -ful to the end of a word to show that something is full of that descriptor				
Adds -less to the end of a word to show that something is without				
Adds re- to the beginning of a word to show it has happened again				
Add additional targets				

Procedure and Data Collection: Run 10-20 trials per session with a **Y** or **N** per trial.
Graph the overall percentage of the number correct on the Per Opportunity Graph.

Mastery Criterion: 80% correct across three consecutive sessions with two different instructors.

Language
Vocabulary Acquisition and Use
L.K.4: L.K.4.a, L.K.4.b
L.K.5: L.K.5.a, L.K.5.b, L.K.5.c, L.K.5.d, L.K.6

STUDENT: _____

L.K.5*

With guidance and support from adults, explore word relationships and nuances in word meanings.

** This standard is divided into four more specified standards: L.K.5.a, L.K.5.b, L.K.5.c, and L.K.5.d.
Once these four standards have been met, L.K.5 is considered mastered.*

L.K.5.a

Sort common objects into categories (e.g., shapes, foods) to gain a sense of the concepts the categories represent.

Materials: *3D Feel and Find, Mighty Mind, All Around Learning Circle Time Activity Set*

Teaching Procedure: Present students with a group of wooden shapes from the *3D Feel and Find*. Model for students how to sort the shapes by color. Let the students try on their own, and then introduce other items for sorting. For some students, you may want to use bowls to show where each color should be sorted.

"Sort." "Which ones belong together?" "Can you put them in like groups?"

TARGET	INTRODUCED	MASTERED	GENERALIZATION PROBE	
When presented with a group of eight objects, sorts objects into two groups based on color				
When presented with a group of 12 objects, sorts objects into three groups based on color				
When presented with a group of eight objects, sorts objects into two groups that have been named by the teacher based on category (For example, teacher asks, "Can you put the vehicles in this bowl and the animals in this bowl?")				
When presented with a group of 12 objects, sorts objects into three groups that have been named by the teacher based on category				
When presented with a group of eight objects, sorts objects into two groups based on category (Student independently chooses categories.)				
When presented with a group of 12 objects, sorts objects into three groups based on category (Student independently chooses categories.)				
When presented with a group of 15 or more objects, sorts objects into three or more categories (Student independently chooses categories.)				
After sorting a group of objects in one way, sorts them in a different way upon request (For example, student initially sorts items by class, and then sorts items by feature such as length or color.)				

Procedure and Data Collection: Run 10-20 trials per session with a **Y** or **N** per trial.
Graph the overall percentage of the number correct on the Per Opportunity Graph.

Mastery Criterion: 80% correct across three consecutive sessions with two different instructors.

Language
Vocabulary Acquisition and Use
L.K.4: L.K.4.a, L.K.4.b
L.K.5: L.K.5.a, L.K.5.b, L.K.5.c, L.K.5.d, L.K.6

STUDENT: _____

L.K.5* With guidance and support from adults, explore word relationships and nuances in word meanings.

** This standard is divided into four more specified standards: L.K.5.a, L.K.5.b, L.K.5.c, and L.K.5.d.
Once these four standards have been met, L.K.5 is considered mastered.*

L.K.5.b Demonstrate understanding of frequently occurring verbs and adjectives by relating them to their opposites (antonyms).

 Materials: *Differentiated Instruction Cubes*

 Teaching Procedure: Prior to this activity, create cards for the *Differentiated Instruction Cubes* using the list of opposites provided for L.K.5.b in Appendix C. Have students take turns rolling the cubes. Students should provide an example or act out each set of opposites. This standard can be supported while reading books or looking at pictures by having students identify examples of opposites within the same picture.

 "What is the opposite of _____?" "Give me an example of _____."

TARGET	INTRODUCED	MASTERED	GENERALIZATION PROBE	
Identifies the opposite of fast and slow				
Identifies the opposite of big and small				
Identifies the opposite of short and tall				
Identifies the opposite of short and long				
Identifies the opposite of clean and dirty				
Identifies the opposite of down and up				
Identifies the opposite of happy and sad				
Identifies the opposite of heavy and light				
Identifies the opposite of new and old				
Relates at least 15 pairs of opposite adjectives				
Identifies the opposite of run and walk				
Identifies the opposite of whisper and yell/shout				
Identifies the opposite of lose and win				
Identifies the opposite of buy and sell				
Relates at least 10 pairs of opposite verbs				

 Procedure and Data Collection: Run 10-20 trials per session with a **Y** or **N** per trial. Graph the overall percentage of the number correct on the Per Opportunity Graph.

Mastery Criterion: 80% correct across three consecutive sessions with two different instructors.

Language
Vocabulary Acquisition and Use
L.K.4: L.K.4.a, L.K.4.b
L.K.5: L.K.5.a, L.K.5.b, L.K.5.c, L.K.5.d, L.K.6

STUDENT: _____

L.K.5* With guidance and support from adults, explore word relationships and nuances in word meanings.

** This standard is divided into four more specified standards: L.K.5.a, L.K.5.b, L.K.5.c, and L.K.5.d.
Once these four standards have been met, L.K.5 is considered mastered.*

L.K.5.c Identify real-life connections between words and their use (e.g., note places at school that are colorful).

Materials: *Differentiated Instruction Cubes*, *What Do You Do With It? ConversaCards*

Teaching Procedure: Prior to this activity, create cards for the *Differentiated Instruction Cubes* using the list of words provided for L.K.5.c in Appendix C. Play this as an "I Spy" game; when the student rolls a word, he/she has to use a complete sentence to describe a space in the environment that fits the description. For students who have mastered this, they can describe a space in *any* environment that fits the description.

"Can you find things that are _____?" "Show me an example of _____."

TARGET	INTRODUCED	MASTERED	GENERALIZATION PROBE	
Identifies items in the environment that are colorful				
Identifies items in the environment that are fun				
Identifies events that are exciting				
Identifies three or more exemplars of 10 or more real-life connections to words				
Identifies three or more exemplars of 25 or more real-life connections to words				
Add additional targets				

Procedure and Data Collection: Run 10-20 trials per session with a **Y** or **N** per trial.
Graph the overall percentage of the number correct on the Per Opportunity Graph.

Mastery Criterion: 80% correct across three consecutive sessions with two different instructors.

Language
Vocabulary Acquisition and Use
L.K.4: L.K.4.a, L.K.4.b
L.K.5: L.K.5.a, L.K.5.b, L.K.5.c, L.K.5.d, L.K.6

STUDENT: _____

L.K.5* With guidance and support from adults, explore word relationships and nuances in word meanings.

** This standard is divided into four more specified standards: L.K.5.a, L.K.5.b, L.K.5.c, and L.K.5.d.
Once these four standards have been met, L.K.5 is considered mastered.*

L.K.5.d Distinguish shades of meaning among verbs describing the same general action (e.g., walk, march, strut, prance) by acting out the meanings.

Materials: *Differentiated Instruction Cubes, I Can Do That! Game*

Teaching Procedure: Prior to this activity, create cards for the *Differentiated Instruction Cubes* using the list of words provided for L.K.5.d in Appendix C. This should be played as an active game. One student rolls a *Differentiated Instruction Cube* then all students must do as instructed. For students who are highly motivated by the *I Can Do That! Game*, you can add your own cards to practice this skill. For example, the game already includes cards that instruct students to crawl, skip, step, and tiptoe. You can add cards such as "march" or "leap."

"Show me what marching looks like." "Show me talking. Now, show me whispering."

TARGET	INTRODUCED	MASTERED	GENERALIZATION PROBE	
Acts out the differences between one set of two verbs that have similar meanings				
Acts out the differences between three sets of two verbs that have similar meanings				
Acts out the differences between five sets of two verbs that have similar meanings				
Acts out the differences between a novel set of two verbs that have similar meanings				
Add additional targets				

Procedure and Data Collection: Run 10-20 trials per session with a **Y** or **N** per trial. Graph the overall percentage of the number correct on the Per Opportunity Graph.

Mastery Criterion: 80% correct across three consecutive sessions with two different instructors.

Language
Vocabulary Acquisition and Use
L.K.4: L.K.4.a, L.K.4.b
L.K.5: L.K.5.a, L.K.5.b, L.K.5.c, L.K.5.d, L.K.6

STUDENT: _____

L.K.6 Use words and phrases acquired through conversations, reading and being read to, and responding to texts.

Materials: *All Around Learning Circle Time Activity Set*, Classroom reading materials, Visual, textual, or gestural prompts during conversation

Teaching Procedure: Prior to a reading activity, select the word(s) you want each student to focus on acquiring during that lesson. Prepare questions in advance for the student to answer using the target word. For example, if your target word is "march," the questions you prepare might look like this: "What did the author say the boy was doing?" (marching) "Can you show me what marching looks like?" Then, while student is marching, say "What are you doing?" "Name a person who marches." During the lesson, ask the questions you have prepared to help each student use the target words and phrases appropriately.

Presentation of a question. "Can you tell me the word from the text?" "Can you describe it better?" "How did the author put it?"

TARGET	INTRODUCED	MASTERED	GENERALIZATION PROBE	
During circle time or story activity, responds to questions using one word or phrase from the activity				
During circle time or story activity, responds to questions using three or more words or phrases from the activity				
During conversations, uses one or more words or phrases introduced in that conversation				
Add additional targets				

Procedure and Data Collection: Run 10-20 trials per session with a **Y** or **N** per trial. Graph the overall percentage of the number correct on the Per Opportunity Graph.

Mastery Criterion: 80% correct across three consecutive sessions with two different instructors.

COUNTING AND CARDINALITY OVERVIEW

· Know number names and the count sequence
· Count to tell the number of objects
· Compare numbers

CCSS CODE	STANDARD
K.CC.A.1	Count to 100 by ones and by tens.
K.CC.A.2	Count forward beginning from a given number within the known sequence (instead of having to begin at 1).
K.CC.A.3	Write numbers from 0 to 20. Represent a number of objects with a written numeral 0-20 (with 0 representing a count of no objects).
K.CC.B.4	Understand the relationship between numbers and quantities; connect counting to cardinality.
K.CC.B.4.a	When counting objects, say the number names in the standard order, pairing each object with one and only one number name and each number name with one and only one object.
K.CC.B.4.b	Understand that the last number name said tells the number of objects counted. The number of objects is the same regardless of their arrangement or the order in which they were counted.
K.CC.B.4.c	Understand that each successive number name refers to a quantity that is one larger.
K.CC.B.5	Count to answer "how many?" questions about as many as 20 things arranged in a line, a rectangular array, or a circle, or as many as 10 things in a scattered configuration; given a number from 1-20, count out that many objects.
K.CC.C.6	Identify whether the number of objects in one group is greater than, less than, or equal to the number of objects in another group, e.g., by using matching and counting strategies.
K.CC.C.7	Compare two numbers between 1 and 10 presented as written numerals.

KIT MATERIALS
· *All Around Learning Circle Time Activity Set*: K.CC.A.1, K.CC.A.2, K.CC.C.7
· *Differentiated Instruction Cubes*: K.CC.A.2, K.CC.C.7
· *Writing and Art Kit*: K.CC.A.3
· *Numbers and Counting Pocket Chart*: K.CC.B.4.a, K.CC.B.5, K.CC.C.7
· *Following Auditory Directions*: K.CC.B.5
· *Math Discovery Kit*: K.CC.B.4.a, K.CC.B.4.b, K.CC.B.4.c, K.CC.B.5, K.CC.C.6, K.CC.C.7
· *Measuring Worms*: K.CC.B.4.b, K.CC.C.6
· *Unifix Cubes*: K.CC.A.1, K.CC.B.4.a, K.CC.B.4.b, K.CC.B.4.c, K.CC.B.5, K.CC.C.6, K.CC.C.7
· *Mathematics with Unifix Cubes*: K.CC.A.1, K.CC.B.4.c, K.CC.B.5, K.CC.C.6, K.CC.C.7

CLASSROOM MATERIALS AND ACTIVITIES

• Number lines

• Math-related storybooks

• Blocks for counting and comparing values

TIP FOR GENERALIZATION

An active generalization game can be played by using masking tape to write the numbers 1-10 and then placing them on different parts of the classroom floor. Students follow directions to move to different numbers (e.g., "Jane, move to a number that is less than six."). It's also easy to differentiate the activity because you can vary the direction based on each student's skill level.

STUDENT: _____

K.CC.A.1   Count to 100 by ones and by tens.

Materials: *All Around Learning Circle Time Activity Set*, *Unifix Cubes, Mathematics with Unifix Cubes*

Teaching Procedure: Let students take turns rolling the inflatable number cubes. After rolling the cube, the student announces the number, and then the whole class starts at 1 and counts up to that number.

"Let's count!" "Can you count with me?" "Count to _____."

TARGET	INTRODUCED	MASTERED	GENERALIZATION PROBE	
Counts to 5 by ones				
Counts to 10 by ones				
Counts to 25 by ones				
Counts to 50 by ones				
Counts to 100 by ones				
Counts to 100 by tens using a number line or other visual cue				
Counts to 100 by tens independently				
Add additional targets				

Procedure and Data Collection: Run 10-20 trials per session with a **Y** or **N** per trial. Graph the overall percentage of the number correct on the Per Opportunity Graph.

Mastery Criterion: 80% correct across three consecutive sessions with two different instructors.

STUDENT: _____

K.CC.A.2 Count forward beginning from a given number within a known sequence (instead of having to begin at 1).

NOTE: This standard requires that students count from a number within a "known sequence." Each student's "known sequence" is determined by their most recently mastered step for K.CC.A.1.

Materials: *Differentiated Instruction Cubes, All Around Learning Circle Time Activity Set*

Teaching Procedure: The *Differentiated Instruction Cubes* are ideal for this activity because you can include numbers on each side of the cube that align with each student's current skill level. Prior to this activity, create cards for the *Differentiated Instruction Cubes* using the list of numbers and symbols provided for K.CC.A.2 in Appendix C. Have students take turns rolling one of the cubes. After rolling, the student must count forward from the number rolled. Some students may need a prompt such as a number line, but prompts should be faded quickly.

"Can you count up starting with _____?" "Count on from _____."

TARGET	INTRODUCED	MASTERED	GENERALIZATION PROBE	
Counts forward from any given number between 1 and 10				
Counts forward from any given number between 1 and 25				
Counts forward from any given number between 1 and 50				
Counts forward from any given number between 1 and 100				
Add additional targets				

Procedure and Data Collection: Run 10-20 trials per session with a **Y** or **N** per trial. Graph the overall percentage of the number correct on the Per Opportunity Graph.

Mastery Criterion: 80% correct across three consecutive sessions with two different instructors.

STUDENT: _____

K.CC.A.3 Write numbers from 0 to 20. Represent a number of objects with a written numeral 0-20 (with 0 representing a count of no objects).

Materials: *Writing and Art Kit*

Teaching Procedure: Provide students with paper and writing utensils from the *Writing and Art Kit*. Model writing the numbers you expect students to print. Allow them time to practice and provide prompts as needed. For learners who find writing activities aversive, provide individualized highly-motivating materials such as different types of paper or writing utensils unique to this activity.

"Write a _____." "Can you make a _____?"

TARGET	INTRODUCED	MASTERED	GENERALIZATION PROBE	
Writes three or more numbers between 0 and 10				
Writes all the numbers between 0 and 10				
Writes a numeral representing the number of objects in a group of one to five objects				
Writes a numeral representing the number of objects in a group of one to 10 objects				
Writes a numeral representing the number of objects in a group of one to 20 objects				
Add additional targets				

Procedure and Data Collection: Run 10-20 trials per session with a **Y** or **N** per trial. Graph the overall percentage of the number correct on the Per Opportunity Graph.

Mastery Criterion: 80% correct across three consecutive sessions with two different instructors.

Counting and Cardinality
Count to Tell the Number of Objects
K.CC.B.4: K.CC.B.4.a, K.CC.B.4.b, K.CC.B.4.c, K.CC.B.5

STUDENT: _____

K.CC.B.4* Understand the relationship between numbers and quantities; connect counting to cardinality.

** This standard is divided into three more specified standards: K.CC.B.4.a, K.CC.B.4.b, and K.CC.B.4.c.
Once these three standards have been met, K.CC.B.4 is considered mastered.*

K.CC.B.4.a When counting objects, say the number names in the standard order, pairing each object with one and only one number name and each number name with one and only one object.

Materials: *Numbers and Counting Pocket Chart, Math Discovery Kit, Unifix Cubes*

Teaching Procedure: Place the object cards from the *Numbers and Counting Pocket Chart* within reach of your students. Give one card to each student and ask them to count how many objects are on that card. When they have correctly counted, you or the students place the object card next to the correct number card on the pocket chart. If students are struggling with counting pictured items, you should have them count objects instead.

"Let's count together." "Can you show me how many are there?"

TARGET	INTRODUCED	MASTERED	GENERALIZATION PROBE	
Counts up to three items with one-to-one correspondence				
Counts up to five items with one-to-one correspondence				
Counts up to 10 items with one-to-one correspondence				
Counts up to 20 items with one-to-one correspondence				
Add additional targets				

Procedure and Data Collection: Run 10-20 trials per session with a **Y** or **N** per trial.
Graph the overall percentage of the number correct on the Per Opportunity Graph.

Mastery Criterion: 80% correct across three consecutive sessions with two different instructors.

Counting and Cardinality
Count to Tell the Number of Objects
**K.CC.B.4: K.CC.B.4.a, K.CC.B.4.b, K.CC.B.4.c,
K.CC.B.5**

STUDENT: _____

K.CC.B.4*

Understand the relationship between numbers and quantities; connect counting to cardinality.

** This standard is divided into three more specified standards: K.CC.B.4.a, K.CC.B.4.b, and K.CC.B.4.c.
Once these three standards have been met, K.CC.B.4 is considered mastered.*

K.CC.B.4.b

Understand that the last number name said tells the number of objects counted. The number of objects is the same regardless of their arrangement or the order in which they were counted.

Materials: *Math Discovery Kit*, *Measuring Worms, Unifix Cubes*

Teaching Procedure: Use the *Comparing Equals* activity mat or the *Counting Objects* activity mat included in the *Math Discovery Kit*. Have students count the items pictured and then place the correct number in the space. If students struggle with counting pictured items, you should have them count objects instead.

"Let's count!" "How many are there?"

TARGET	INTRODUCED	MASTERED	GENERALIZATION PROBE	
Counts three or more items, and then responds correctly to "How many?"				
After responding to "How many?" correctly for three or more items, responds correctly when teacher rearranges items and re-asks, "How many?"				
Counts five or more items, and then responds correctly to "How many?"				
After responding to "How many?" correctly for five or more items, responds correctly when teacher rearranges items and re-asks, "How many?"				
Counts 10 or more items, and then responds correctly to "How many?"				
After responding to "How many?" correctly for 10 or more items, responds correctly when teacher rearranges items and re-asks, "How many?"				
Add additional targets				

Procedure and Data Collection: Run 10-20 trials per session with a **Y** or **N** per trial.
Graph the overall percentage of the number correct on the Per Opportunity Graph.

Mastery Criterion: 80% correct across three consecutive sessions with two different instructors.

Counting and Cardinality
Count to Tell the Number of Objects
K.CC.B.4: K.CC.B.4.a, K.CC.B.4.b, K.CC.B.4.c, K.CC.B.5

STUDENT: _____

K.CC.B.4*

Understand the relationship between numbers and quantities; connect counting to cardinality.

* This standard is divided into three more specified standards: K.CC.B.4.a, K.CC.B.4.b, and K.CC.B.4.c. Once these three standards have been met, K.CC.B.4 is considered mastered.

K.CC.B.4.c

Understand that each successive number name refers to a quantity that is one larger.

Materials: *Math Discovery Kit, Unifix Cubes, Mathematics with Unifix Cubes*

Teaching Procedure: Use the color circle counters from the *Math Discovery Kit*. Place one on the table in view of all students. Ask, "How many?" Place a second counter and ask, "Now, how many?" Continue in this way until five counters have been placed. Have students practice on their own with counters or other objects. You may want to consider using the *Comparing Equals* activity mat from the kit, placing counters in the circles on that mat to provide a clearer visual representation for students.

"How many are there if I add one more?" "What is one bigger?"

TARGET	INTRODUCED	MASTERED	GENERALIZATION PROBE	
After counting a group of one to three objects, answers correctly if the teacher asks, "How many are there now?" while adding one more object				
After stating a number between 1 and 3, answers correctly if the teachers asks a question such as, "What is one bigger?"				
After counting a group of four to 10 objects, answers correctly if the teacher asks, "How many are there now?" while adding one more object				
After stating a number between 4 and 10, answers correctly if the teachers asks a question such as, "What is one bigger?"				
Add additional targets				

Procedure and Data Collection: Run 10-20 trials per session with a **Y** or **N** per trial. Graph the overall percentage of the number correct on the Per Opportunity Graph.

Mastery Criterion: 80% correct across three consecutive sessions with two different instructors.

Counting and Cardinality
Count to Tell the Number of Objects
K.CC.B.4: K.CC.B.4.a, K.CC.B.4.b, K.CC.B.4.c, K.CC.B.5

STUDENT: _____

K.CC.B.5

Count to answer "how many?" questions about as many as 20 things arranged in a line, a rectangular array, or a circle, or as many as 10 things in a scattered configuration; given a number from 1-20, count out that many objects.

Materials: *Math Discovery Kit, Following Auditory Directions, Numbers and Counting Pocket Chart, Unifix Cubes, Mathematics with Unifix Cubes*

Teaching Procedure: Place the square rubber tiles from the *Math Discovery Kit* with lines and arrays of pictured items on the table in view of all students. Practice counting the items pictured. If students struggle with counting pictured items, you can have them count objects instead. If students have mastered counting items arranged in a line or an array, use the color circle counters arranged in a scattered configuration to practice more complex counting skills.

"Let's count!" "Can you give me _____ items?" "Count to _____."

TARGET	INTRODUCED	MASTERED	GENERALIZATION PROBE	
Counts up to five items when arranged in a line				
Counts up to five items when arranged in a rectangular array or a circle				
Counts up to five items when arranged in a scattered configuration				
Counts up to 10 items when arranged in a line				
Counts up to 10 items when arranged in a rectangular array or a circle				
Counts up to 10 items when arranged in a scattered configuration				
Counts up to 20 items when arranged in a line				
Counts up to 20 items when arranged in a rectangular array or a circle				
When given a number between 1 and 3, counts out that number of objects				
When given a number between 4 and 10, counts out that number of objects				
When given a number between 11 and 20, counts out that number of objects				

Procedure and Data Collection: Run 10-20 trials per session with a **Y** or **N** per trial. Graph the overall percentage of the number correct on the Per Opportunity Graph.

Mastery Criterion: 80% correct across three consecutive sessions with two different instructors.

K.CC.C.6 Identify whether the number of objects in one group is greater than, less than, or equal to the number of objects in another group, e.g., by using matching and counting strategies.

 Materials: *Math Discovery Kit*, *Unifix Cubes*, *Mathematics with Unifix Cubes*, *Measuring Worms*

 Teaching Procedure: Place two square rubber tiles from the *Math Discovery Kit* with pictured items on the table in view of all students. Model for the students how you count the number of items on each tile, then let students practice on their own with prompting and support. In order to teach a matching strategy, you must have groups of objects to compare or groups of objects pictured on paper on which the student can write. Match an object from one group to an object in the other group. Continue matching until you are unable to make a match, then identify which group has objects remaining and label it as having "more" than the other group. If you're using paper, cross out one item from each group, then continue crossing out pairs of items until only one group has items remaining. For students who have mastered these steps and are motivated by number work, you can introduce the "greater than" and "less than" yellow activity mats from the *Math Discovery Kit*.

S^D "Which one has more?" "Do these two groups have the same amount?"

TARGET	INTRODUCED	MASTERED	GENERALIZATION PROBE	
Compares two groups of up to five items by matching items, and then tells which group has more or less				
Compares two groups of up to 10 items by matching items, and then tells which group has more or less				
Compares two groups of up to five items by counting the items in each group, and then tells which group has more or less				
Compares two groups of up to 10 items by counting the items in each group, and then tells which group has more or less				
Identifies when two groups of items have equal amounts				
Add additional targets				

 Procedure and Data Collection: Run 10-20 trials per session with a **Y** or **N** per trial. Graph the overall percentage of the number correct on the Per Opportunity Graph.

Mastery Criterion: 80% correct across three consecutive sessions with two different instructors.

STUDENT: _____

K.CC.C.7 Compare two numbers between 1 and 10 presented as written numerals.

NOTE: K.CC.C.6 should be mastered prior to introducing this standard.

Materials: *Math Discovery Kit, Differentiated Instruction Cubes, Numbers and Counting Pocket Chart, All Around Learning Circle Time Activity Set, Unifix Cubes, Mathematics with Unifix Cubes*

Teaching Procedure: Place two square rubber number tiles from the *Math Discovery Kit* on the table in view of all students. Model for the students how you recognize that one number is more than another number. You can use a number line or visual strategy such as drawing dots to count out each number. Then let students practice on their own with prompting and support. For students who have mastered these steps and are motivated by number work, you can introduce the *greater than* and *less than* yellow activity mats from the kit. Refer to K.CC.C.7 in Appendix C for instructions for a customized game using the *Differentiated Instruction Cubes* to practice comparing numbers.

"Which number is bigger?" "Compare these two numbers."

TARGET	INTRODUCED	MASTERED	GENERALIZATION PROBE	
Compares two numbers between 1 and 10 presented as written numerals, grouping objects to represent the numbers				
Compares two numbers between 1 and 10 presented as written numerals without any visual prompts				
Add additional targets				

Procedure and Data Collection: Run 10-20 trials per session with a **Y** or **N** per trial. Graph the overall percentage of the number correct on the Per Opportunity Graph.

Mastery Criterion: 80% correct across three consecutive sessions with two different instructors.

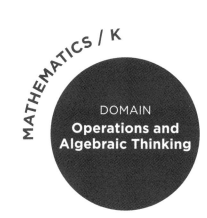

OPERATIONS AND ALGEBRAIC THINKING OVERVIEW

· Understand addition as putting together and adding to
· Understand subtraction as taking apart and taking from

CCSS CODE	STANDARD
K.OA.A.1	Represent addition and subtraction with objects, fingers, mental images, drawings, sounds (e.g., claps), acting out situations, verbal explanations, expressions, or equations.
K.OA.A.2	Solve addition and subtraction word problems, and add and subtract within 10, e.g., by using objects or drawings to represent the problem.
K.OA.A.3	Decompose numbers less than or equal to 10 into pairs in more than one way, e.g., by using objects or drawings, and record each decomposition by a drawing or equation (e.g., 5 = 2 + 3 and 5 = 4 + 1).
K.OA.A.4	For any number from 1 to 9, find the number that makes 10 when added to the given number, e.g., by using objects or drawings, and record the answer with a drawing or equation.
K.OA.A.5	Fluently add and subtract within 5.

KIT MATERIALS

· *Measuring Worms*: K.OA.A.1, K.OA.A.2
· *Math Discovery Kit*: K.OA.A.1, K.OA.A.2, K.OA.A.5
· *Unifix Cubes*: K.OA.A.1, K.OA.A.2, K.OA.A.3, K.OA.A.4
· *Mathematics with Unifix Cubes*: K.OA.A.3
· *Numbers and Counting Pocket Chart*: K.OA.A.2, K.OA.A.4, K.OA.A.5
· *All Around Learning Circle Time Activity Set*: K.OA.A.5
· *Inchimals*: K.OA.A.1, K.OA.A.4, K.OA.A.5

CLASSROOM MATERIALS AND ACTIVITIES

· Common objects in the classroom
· Community walk to find groups of 10
· Math-related stories
· Math workbooks

TIP FOR GENERALIZATION

A fun activity for composing numbers is to use dominoes and challenge your students to find all the dominoes that add up to a specific number. Students should be able to explain how the two numbers represented on the dominoes compose the number. For example, if you tell students to find dominoes that add up to nine, students should be able to show that 3 dots plus 6 dots equals 9 dots.

Operations and Algebraic Thinking
Understand Addition, and
Understand Subtraction
K.OA.A.1, K.OA.A.2, K.OA.A.3, K.OA.A.4, K.OA.A.5

STUDENT: _____

K.OA.A.1

Represent addition and subtraction with objects, fingers, mental images, drawings,* sounds (e.g., claps), acting out situations, verbal explanations, expressions, or equations.

Drawings need not show details, but should show the mathematics in the problem. (This applies wherever drawings are mentioned in the Standard)

Materials: *Measuring Worms, Inchimals, Math Discovery Kit, Unifix Cubes*

Teaching Procedure: Organize students into pairs. Give each student in the pair a small number of worms. Each student counts their worms, and then the two students work together to find the sum. They can draw, write, or dictate the math problem. There are also addition and subtraction activities included in the *Math Discovery Kit* and *Inchimals* activity book.

"Let's add." "What is _____ + _____?" "Can we figure this out?"

TARGET	INTRODUCED	MASTERED	GENERALIZATION PROBE	
Uses objects or fingers to represent addition				
Uses drawings to represent addition				
Uses objects or fingers to represent subtraction				
Uses drawings to represent subtraction				
Represents addition with a written equation				
Represents subtraction with a written equation				
Add additional targets				

Procedure and Data Collection: Run 10-20 trials per session with a **Y** or **N** per trial. Graph the overall percentage of the number correct on the Per Opportunity Graph.

Mastery Criterion: 80% correct across three consecutive sessions with two different instructors.

STUDENT: _____

K.OA.A.2 Solve addition and subtraction word problems, and add and subtract within 10, e.g., by using objects or drawings to represent the problem.

Materials: *Numbers and Counting Pocket Chart, Measuring Worms, Math Discovery Kit, Unifix Cubes*

Teaching Procedure: Use the addition and subtraction cards included in the *Numbers and Counting Pocket Chart* to illustrate simple word problems. The cards included in the kit use both images and numbers to show addition and subtraction problems, so you can choose the format that is most appropriate for your students' current skill level. Place a card in the pocket chart, and then tell a brief story. For example, place the card that has *one bear + two bears* and say, "One bear was walking in the forest. Two more bears started walking with him. How many bears are there altogether?" Then have students solve the problem and place the correct picture card in the chart to complete the equation.

"Let's solve the problem." "Can you figure out the answer?" Presentation of problem.

TARGET	INTRODUCED	MASTERED	GENERALIZATION PROBE	
Solve addition word problems within 5 that include simple, direct sentences (For example, Jenny had one balloon. Her mom gave her two more balloons. How many does she have?)				
Solve addition word problems within 10 that include simple, direct sentences (For example, Jenny had 7 balloons. Her mom gave her two more balloons. How many does she have?)				
Solve subtraction word problems within 5 that include simple, direct sentences (For example, Jenny had two balloons. Her mom took one balloon away. How many does she have?)				
Solve subtraction word problems within 10 that include simple, direct sentences (For example, Jenny had nine balloons. Her mom took one balloon away. How many does she have?)				
Add additional targets				

Procedure and Data Collection: Run 10-20 trials per session with a **Y** or **N** per trial. Graph the overall percentage of the number correct on the Per Opportunity Graph.

Mastery Criterion: 80% correct across three consecutive sessions with two different instructors.

K.OA.A.3

Decompose numbers less than or equal to 10 into pairs in more than one way, e.g., by using objects or drawings, and record each decomposition by a drawing or equation (e.g., 5 = 2 + 3 and 5 = 4 + 1).

Materials: *Unifix Cubes*, *Mathematics with Unifix Cubes*

Teaching Procedure: Give each student several cubes in two colors. Have them compose a given number in as many ways as they can using the cubes. For example, if a student has blue and red cubes and the given number is 5, they can attach 1 blue cube to 4 red cubes, 2 blue cubes to 3 red cubes, and so on. They can draw, write, or dictate the math problems.

"Show me two ways to make five." "How many ways can you make six?"

TARGET	INTRODUCED	MASTERED	GENERALIZATION PROBE	
Decomposes numbers less than or equal to 5 into pairs in more than one way using objects				
Decomposes numbers less than or equal to 10 into pairs in more than one way using objects				
Decomposes numbers less than or equal to 5 into pairs in more than one way using a drawing or an equation				
Decomposes numbers less than or equal to 10 into pairs in more than one way using a drawing or an equation				
Add additional targets				

Procedure and Data Collection: Run 10-20 trials per session with a **Y** or **N** per trial. Graph the overall percentage of the number correct on the Per Opportunity Graph.

Mastery Criterion: 80% correct across three consecutive sessions with two different instructors.

Operations and Algebraic Thinking
Understand Addition, and
Understand Subtraction
K.OA.A.1, K.OA.A.2, K.OA.A.3, K.OA.A.4, K.OA.A.5

K.OA.A.4 For any number from 1 to 9, find the number that makes 10 when added to the given number, e.g., by using objects or drawings, and record the answer with a drawing or equation.

Materials: *Inchimals, Numbers and Counting Pocket Chart, Unifix Cubes*

Teaching Procedure: Place the ostrich block standing up on the table. Explain that the ostrich is 10 inches tall. You can count the hash marks on the side of the ostrich, and then show the students the 10 at the top of the ostrich. Now stand the ape block up next to the ostrich. Show students that it is 9 inches. Place the ladybug, frog, and mouse on the table and ask students which one you should stack on top of the ape to make it the same height as the ostrich. Then have students work together to stack different animals up to equal the height of the ostrich. They can write, draw, or dictate each equation they create. (For example, when they stack the ladybug on the ape, they can write 9 + 1 = 10.)

"Can you make ten?" "What can you add to 8 to make 10?"

TARGET	INTRODUCED	MASTERED	GENERALIZATION PROBE	
Uses objects to make 10 when given any number 1 through 9				
Uses objects to make 10 when given any number 1 through 9, then records answer using drawing or equations				
Add additional targets				

Procedure and Data Collection: Run 10-20 trials per session with a **Y** or **N** per trial. Graph the overall percentage of the number correct on the Per Opportunity Graph.

Mastery Criterion: 80% correct across three consecutive sessions with two different instructors.

Operations and Algebraic Thinking
Understand Addition, and
Understand Subtraction
K.OA.A.1, K.OA.A.2, K.OA.A.3, K.OA.A.4, K.OA.A.5

STUDENT: _____

K.OA.A.5   Fluently add and subtract within 5.

Materials: *All Around Learning Circle Time Activity Set*, *Math Discovery Kit, Inchimals, Numbers and Counting Pocket Chart*

Teaching Procedure: Use the *All Around Learning Circle Time Activity Set* as a part of your daily routine. Have students stand on a certain number, and then ask them to show "plus two" or "minus three" by moving to the sum or difference. For example, if a student is standing on the 9 and you ask them to find the difference for 9 - 3, they should move three steps to the 6.

"What's the answer?" "Can you solve it?" Presentation of problem.

TARGET	INTRODUCED	MASTERED	GENERALIZATION PROBE	
Fluently adds within 5				
Fluently subtracts within 5				
Fluently responds to a random rotation of addition and subtraction questions within 5				
Add additional targets				

Procedure and Data Collection: Run 10-20 trials per session with a **Y** or **N** per trial. Graph the overall percentage of the number correct on the Per Opportunity Graph.

Mastery Criterion: 80% correct across three consecutive sessions with two different instructors.

DOMAIN
Numbers and Operations in Base Ten

NUMBER AND OPERATIONS IN BASE TEN OVERVIEW

· Work with numbers 11-19 to gain foundations for place value

CCSS CODE	STANDARD
K.NBT.A.1	Compose and decompose numbers from 11 to 19 into ten ones and some further ones, e.g., by using objects or drawings, and record each composition or decomposition by a drawing or equation (such as 18 = 10 + 8); understand that these numbers are composed of ten ones and one, two, three, four, five, six, seven, eight, or nine ones.

KIT MATERIALS

· *Unifix Cubes*: K.NBT.A.1
· *Inchimals*: K.NBT.A.1

CLASSROOM MATERIALS AND ACTIVITIES

· Drawings of numbers
· Popsicle sticks
· Pennies and dimes

TIP FOR GENERALIZATION

On the first day of school, start an activity for counting the first 100 days of school. Label two jars as ONES and TENS. Place them on a shelf or wall where they are clearly visible. Each day, have a student add a popsicle stick to the ONES jar, then count all the popsicle sticks. When there are ten popsicle sticks in the ONES jar, wrap a rubber band around them and move them to the TENS jar. Continue counting daily until the hundredth day of school. Not all of your students will be able to comprehend the concept of TENS, but you can assign each student jobs related to this activity that are appropriate for his/her current skill level.

Numbers and Operations in Base Ten
Work with Numbers 11-19 to Gain
Foundations for Place Value
K.NBT.A.1

STUDENT: _____

K.NBT.A.1 Compose and decompose numbers from 11 to 19 into ten ones and some further ones, e.g., by using objects or drawings, and record each composition or decomposition by a drawing or equation (such as 18 = 10 + 8); understand that these numbers are composed of ten ones and one, two, three, four, five, six, seven, eight, or nine ones.

Prerequisite skill: Students should be able to count, write, and recognize the numbers 1 through 19.

 Materials: *Unifix Cubes, Inchimals*

 Teaching Procedure: Give each student ten cubes in one color. Have them put all ten together to create a "ten stick." Then, give each student ten cubes in a second color. Model how you compose a number between 11 and 19. For example, write the number 14 and show students that you make 14 by putting your "ten stick" with four single cubes. Challenge students to compose and discuss several numbers between 11 and 19 using the cubes.

 "What are the parts of this number?" "Can you trade your ones for a ten?" "Are these the same?" "How can you make this number?" "Draw this number for me."

TARGET	INTRODUCED	MASTERED	GENERALIZATION PROBE	
Can "bundle" or "trade" 10 ones into one 10				
Demonstrates understanding that one 10 is the same as 10 ones				
Composes a number using one 10 and the appropriate number of ones (For example, composes 14 by using one 10 and four ones using manipulatives or drawings.)				
Decomposes a number using tens and ones (For example, decomposes 14 by separating one ten and four ones using manipulatives or drawings.)				
Makes a drawing of a number (For example, draws 10 circles in one box and four in another box to make 14.)				
Writes the equation for a number after using manipulatives or drawing to create it (For example, draws 10 circles in one box and four in another box to make 14 then writes 10 + 4 = 14 underneath it.)				
Add additional targets				

 Procedure and Data Collection: Run 10-20 trials per session with a **Y** or **N** per trial. Graph the overall percentage of the number correct on the Per Opportunity Graph.

Mastery Criterion: 80% correct across three consecutive sessions with two different instructors.

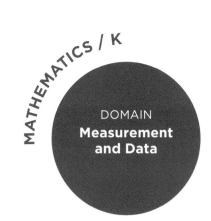

DOMAIN
Measurement and Data

MEASUREMENT AND DATA OVERVIEW

• Describe and compare measurable attributes
• Classify objects and count the number of objects in each category

CCSS CODE	STANDARD
K.MD.A.1	Describe measurable attributes of objects, such as length or weight. Describe several measurable attributes of a single object.
K.MD.A.2	Directly compare two objects with a measurable attribute in common, to see which object has "more of"/"less of" the attribute, and describe the difference. For example, directly compare the heights of two children and describe one child as taller/shorter.
K.MD.B.3	Classify objects into given categories; count the numbers of objects in each category and sort the categories by count.

KIT MATERIALS

• *Inchimals*: K.MD.A.1, K.MD.A.2
• *3D Feel and Find*: K.MD.A.1, K.MD.A.2, K.MD.B.3
• *Measuring Worms*: K.MD.A.1, K.MD.A.2, K.MD.B.3
• *Following Auditory Directions*: K.MD.A.2
• *Mighty Mind*: K.MD.B.3
• *Unifix Cubes*: K.MD.A.1, K.MD.A.2
• *Mathematics with Unifix Cubes*: K.MD.A.1, K.MD.A.2

CLASSROOM MATERIALS AND ACTIVITIES

• Balance/scale
• Height measurements of peers

TIP FOR GENERALIZATION

Go on a community walk. Compare the heights of buildings or trees, compare the number of windows on two buildings, count the number of blue cars you see, etc.

STUDENT: _____

K.MD.A.1 Describe measurable attributes of objects, such as length or weight. Describe several measurable attributes of a single object.

Materials: *Measuring Worms, Inchimals, 3D Feel and Find, Unifix Cubes, Mathematics with Unifix Cubes*

Teaching Procedure: Give each student several *Measuring Worms*. Have them compare worms using appropriate vocabulary such as "long" and "short." If students are struggling with this, you should provide and sort several examples and non-examples. For example, you may teach the concept by having two boxes on the table, one labeled "long" and the other labeled "short." Then hold up a measuring worm, state "short" and put it in the box for "short." Continue this with several examples, and then have students try.

"Is _____ long or short?" "Is this item short or tall?" (Be sure to mix up the order the options are presented.) "Tell me about _____."

TARGET	INTRODUCED	MASTERED	GENERALIZATION PROBE	
Responds correctly to "Is _____ long or short?"				
Responds correctly to "Is _____ heavy or light?"				
Responds correctly to "Is _____ tall or short?"				
Responds correctly to "Is _____ full or empty?"				
Finds long and short items in the environment				
Finds heavy and light items in the environment				
Finds tall and short items in the environment				
Finds full and empty items in the environment				
Describes an item as "long" or "short"				
Describes an item as "heavy" or "light"				
Describes an item as "tall" or "short"				
Describes an item as "full" or "empty"				
Add additional targets				

Procedure and Data Collection: Run 10-20 trials per session with a **Y** or **N** per trial. Graph the overall percentage of the number correct on the Per Opportunity Graph.

Mastery Criterion: 80% correct across three consecutive sessions with two different instructors.

STUDENT: _____

K.MD.A.2 Directly compare two objects with a measurable attribute in common, to see which object has "more of"/"less of" the attribute, and describe the difference. For example, directly compare the heights of two children and describe one child as taller/shorter.

NOTE: Student must have mastered L.K.5.b prior to introducing this standard.

Materials: *Inchimals, Measuring Worms, 3D Feel and Find, Unifix Cubes, Mathematics with Unifix Cubes, Following Auditory Directions*

Teaching Procedure: Place two of the *Inchimal* blocks on the table and model how you compare them using the terms "taller" and "shorter." It can be beneficial to add both visual cues (such as stretching out your hands for "taller" and pinching your fingers together for "shorter") as well as auditory cues (such as stretching out the word "taaaaaller"). Provide multiple examples for students to explore and describe with prompting.

"Compare these two items." "Compare the _____ with the _____." "Which has more?"

TARGET	INTRODUCED	MASTERED	GENERALIZATION PROBE	
Compares two objects by length using the words "longer" and "shorter"				
Compares two objects by weight using the words "heavier" or "lighter"				
Compares two objects by height using the words "taller" or "shorter"				
Compares two objects using the words "more" or "less" (such as "This one has more sides")				
Add additional targets				

Procedure and Data Collection: Run 10-20 trials per session with a **Y** or **N** per trial. Graph the overall percentage of the number correct on the Per Opportunity Graph.

Mastery Criterion: 80% correct across three consecutive sessions with two different instructors.

STUDENT: _____

K.MD.B.3 Classify objects into given categories; count the numbers of objects in each category and sort the categories by count.*

* Limit category counts to be less than or equal to 10.

Materials: *Mighty Mind, Measuring Worms, 3D Feel and Find*

Teaching Procedure: Present students with a group of tiles from *Mighty Mind*. Model for students how to sort the shapes by color. Let the students try on their own, and then introduce other items for sorting. For some students, you may want to use bowls to show where each color should be sorted.

"Sort." "Where do they belong?" "Put them in groups that are the same."

TARGET	INTRODUCED	MASTERED	GENERALIZATION PROBE	
Sorts objects into two groups by color				
Sorts objects into four groups by color				
Sorts objects into four groups by color with extra objects present				
Sorts objects into two groups by size				
Sorts objects into four groups by size				
Sorts objects into four groups by size with extra objects present				
Sorts objects into groups by function (i.e., things you find in a bedroom, living room, and kitchen)				
Sorts objects into groups by feature (i.e., shapes with 3 sides, 4 sides, and more than 4 sides OR objects that are short, medium, and tall)				
Sorts the same group of items in two different ways (i.e., sorts items by color, then sorts items by size)				
Once items have been sorted, counts the objects in each category and tells which group has the most items				
Once items have been sorted, counts the objects in each category and tells which group has the least items				
Once items have been sorted, counts the objects in each category and arranges groups from smallest to largest number of objects				

Procedure and Data Collection: Run 10-20 trials per session with a **Y** or **N** per trial. Graph the overall percentage of the number correct on the Per Opportunity Graph.

Mastery Criterion: 80% correct across three consecutive sessions with two different instructors.

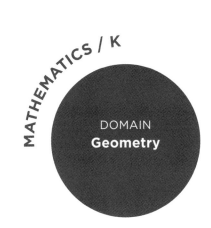

GEOMETRY OVERVIEW

- Identify and describe shapes
- Analyze, compare, create, and compose shapes

CCSS CODE	STANDARD
K.G.A.1	Describe objects in the environment using names of shapes, and describe the relative positions of these objects using terms such as above, below, beside, in front of, behind, and next to.
K.G.A.2	Correctly name shapes regardless of their orientations or overall size.
K.G.A.3	Identify shapes as two-dimensional (lying in a plane, "flat") or three-dimensional ("solid").
K.G.B.4	Analyze and compare two- and three-dimensional shapes, in different sizes and orientations, using informal language to describe their similarities, differences, parts and other attributes.
K.G.B.5	Model shapes in the world by building shapes from components and drawing shapes.
K.G.B.6	Compose simple shapes to form larger shapes.

KIT MATERIALS

- *I Can Do That! Game*: K.G.A.1
- *Following Auditory Directions*: K.G.A.1
- *Mighty Mind*: K.G.A.2, K.G.B.4, K.G.B.6
- *All Around Learning Circle Time Activity Set*: K.G.A.2, K.G.B.4
- *3D Feel and Find*: K.G.A.3

CLASSROOM MATERIALS AND ACTIVITIES

- Teacher- or student-created shapes
- Tangrams
- 3D shapes from a shape sorter
- Shape puzzles
- Modeling materials: clay, straw, toothpicks, etc.

TIP FOR GENERALIZATION

Give each student a container with four to five different shapes (printed on cards, shape blocks, shape puzzle pieces, etc.). Put a shape in the center of the table. Each student must find one shape in their box that has one thing in common with the shape in the middle. The shapes can be the same size, both be 2D or 3D, they can share the same number of sides, etc. It's a great group activity because everyone is playing simultaneously.

K.G.A.1 Describe objects in the environment using names of shapes, and describe the relative positions of these objects using terms such as *above, below, beside, in front of, behind,* and *next to.*

 Materials: *I Can Do That! Game, Following Auditory Directions*

 Teaching Procedure: Play *I Can Do That!* as a fun way to introduce and model prepositions. The game requires students to pick three cards that provide instructions using prepositions. You may want to modify the game to include fewer cards while still using the motivating materials to practice using prepositions.

 "Tell me about _____." "Where is it?" "What is it?"

TARGET	INTRODUCED	MASTERED	GENERALIZATION PROBE	
Describes three different objects in the environment by naming its shape				
Describes 10 different objects in the environment by naming its shape				
Describes 25 different objects in the environment by naming its shape				
Describes novel objects in the environment by naming its shape				
Describes the relative position of an object using the term "above"				
Describes the relative position of an object using the term "below"				
Describes the relative position of an object using the term "beside"				
Describes the relative position of an object using the term "in front of"				
Describes the relative position of an object using the term "behind"				
Describes the relative position of an object using the term "next to"				
Describes the relative position of an object using the term "inside"				
Describes the relative position of an object using the term "on top of"				
Describes the relative position of an object using the term "on"				

 Procedure and Data Collection: Run 10-20 trials per session with a **Y** or **N** per trial. Graph the overall percentage of the number correct on the Per Opportunity Graph.

Mastery Criterion: 80% correct across three consecutive sessions with two different instructors.

STUDENT: _____

 K.G.A.2 Correctly name shapes regardless of their orientations or overall size.

 Materials: *Mighty Mind, All Around Learning Circle Time Activity Set*

 Teaching Procedure: Present each of the students with one of the tiles from *Mighty Mind*. Have each student name the shape. Once students have named the shape, present another example of the same shape. Do this multiple times with many different examples of the shape in different orientations and sizes. Then have students do a shape scavenger hunt. If you've been working on identifying circles, have them move around the classroom or look in a book to find as many circles as they can.

S^D "What is this?" "What is it called?" "This is a _____." Presentation of the shape.

TARGET	INTRODUCED	MASTERED	GENERALIZATION PROBE	
Identifies a circle				
Identifies a square				
Identifies a triangle				
Identifies a diamond				
Identifies a rectangle				
Identifies an oval				
Identifies a star				
Identifies a crescent				
Identifies a heart				
Identifies a pentagon				
Identifies an octagon				
Add additional targets				

 Procedure and Data Collection: Run 10-20 trials per session with a **Y** or **N** per trial. Graph the overall percentage of the number correct on the Per Opportunity Graph.

Mastery Criterion: 80% correct across three consecutive sessions with two different instructors.

STUDENT: _____

K.G.A.3 Identify shapes as two-dimensional (lying in a plane, "flat") or three-dimensional ("solid").

NOTE: Student must have mastered K.G.A.2 prior to introducing this standard.

Materials: *3D Feel and Find*, Drawings of 2D shapes, Classroom books that include 2D shapes

Teaching Procedure: Make several examples of 2D and 3D shapes available. Show one shape from the *3D Feel and Find* and one shape drawn on paper. Talk about how they are different, using the words "solid" and "flat." Have students find and identify examples of solid and flat shapes.

"Is this flat or solid?" "Is this solid or flat?" "Tell me about this shape."

TARGET	INTRODUCED	MASTERED	GENERALIZATION PROBE	
Identifies a 2D shape as "flat" when presented in a field of 2D and 3D shapes				
Identifies a 3D shape as "solid" when presented in a field of 2D and 3D shapes				
Identifies a cylinder				
Identifies a pyramid				
Identifies a cube				
Identifies a sphere				
Identifies a cone				
Add additional targets				

Procedure and Data Collection: Run 10-20 trials per session with a **Y** or **N** per trial. Graph the overall percentage of the number correct on the Per Opportunity Graph.

Mastery Criterion: 80% correct across three consecutive sessions with two different instructors.

STUDENT: _____

K.G.B.4

Analyze and compare two- and three-dimensional shapes, in different sizes and orientations, using informal language to describe their similarities, differences, parts (e.g., number of sides and vertices/"corners") and other attributes (e.g., having sides of equal length).

Materials: *All Around Learning Circle Time Activity Set*, *Mighty Mind*

Teaching Procedure: Use the *All Around Learning Circle Time Activity Set* as a part of your daily routine. Have students stand on a shape on the mat. Instruct one student to describe an attribute of his/her shape, and then have other students respond with the attributes of their own shapes. For example, the first student might say, "I'm on the diamond. It has four sides." Then, all other students share how many sides their shapes have.

"What is the same about these two shapes?" "What is different about these two shapes?"
"Compare these shapes."

TARGET	INTRODUCED	MASTERED	GENERALIZATION PROBE	
Compares by size (big/small)				
Compares by number of sides				
Compares by number of corners				
Compares by 2D or 3D				
Compares by sides of equal lengths or different lengths				
Add additional targets				

Procedure and Data Collection: Run 10-20 trials per session with a **Y** or **N** per trial. Graph the overall percentage of the number correct on the Per Opportunity Graph.

Mastery Criterion: 80% correct across three consecutive sessions with two different instructors.

STUDENT: _____

K.G.B.5 Model shapes in the world by building shapes from components (e.g., sticks and clay balls) and drawing shapes.

Materials: Clay, toothpicks, straws, and other building materials (not included in kit)

Teaching Procedure: Prior to the lesson, create a sample of a prism using toothpicks and balls of play dough. Use the balls of play dough to connect the toothpicks and create the shape. Give students play dough and toothpicks and ask them to recreate your sample. After a student has created the prism, challenge them to create other shapes such as cubes, pyramids, and tetrahedron.

"Can you make a _____?" "Show me a _____." "What does a _____ look like?"

TARGET	INTRODUCED	MASTERED	GENERALIZATION PROBE	
Traces three shapes				
Traces eight shapes				
Draws three shapes				
Draws eight shapes				
Creates three 3D shapes using play dough				
Creates three 3D shapes using building materials (such as blocks, straws, etc.)				
Add additional targets				

Procedure and Data Collection: Run 10-20 trials per session with a **Y** or **N** per trial. Graph the overall percentage of the number correct on the Per Opportunity Graph.

Mastery Criterion: 80% correct across three consecutive sessions with two different instructors.

STUDENT: _____

K.G.B.6

Compose simple shapes to form larger shapes. For example, *"Can you join these two triangles with full sides touching to make a rectangle?"*

Materials: *Mighty Mind*

Teaching Procedure: Present students with the shapes required to create a larger shape. For example, you can present each student with two triangles and challenge them to make a diamond. For some students, you may want to trace an outline of the diamond shape as a visual cue to assist them in completing the task. For other students who excel in this area, you may want to provide additional shapes for them to choose from in order to make the activity more challenging.

"Use these shapes to make a rectangle." "Can you make a bigger shape out of these shapes?"

TARGET	INTRODUCED	MASTERED	GENERALIZATION PROBE	
Creates a diamond using two triangles				
Creates a rectangle using two squares				
Creates a square using two triangles				
Creates a pentagon using a square and a triangle				
Creates large shapes using three smaller shapes				
Creates multiple shapes using the *Mighty Mind* cards or similar cards				
Add additional targets				

Procedure and Data Collection: Run 10-20 trials per session with a **Y** or **N** per trial.
Graph the overall percentage of the number correct on the Per Opportunity Graph.

Mastery Criterion: 80% correct across three consecutive sessions with two different instructors.

APPENDIX

A

Preference Assessment

Preference Assessment

Conducting a preference assessment for each student should be one of the first things you do. Having a clear understanding of what items and activities are highly motivating for your student will provide opportunities to reinforce for correct responses and adaptive behavior.

To conduct a preference assessment, place many toys and objects around a room and watch how the student interacts with them for about 20-30 minutes. If you have a student with poor scanning skills, you can present items two at a time and see what the learner reaches for.

You will make several presentations of items to the student, arranging them in different groupings. As you are observing, place tally marks in the charts below to easily recognize patterns. When you have completed the assessment, fill in the final page to have a comprehensive list of reinforcing items and activities.

VISUAL STIMULI				
STIMULUS	PICKED FIRST FROM ARRAY OF 3-5 ITEMS	INTERACTED WITH FOR ONE OR MORE MINUTES	INTERACTED WITH FOR FIVE OR MORE MINUTES	REQUESTED WHEN ITEM WAS NOT PRESENT OR OUT OF SIGHT
Light up toy				
Spinning toy (i.e., top)				
Jigsaw puzzle				
Stickers				

TACTILE STIMULI				
STIMULUS	PICKED FIRST FROM ARRAY OF 3-5 ITEMS	INTERACTED WITH FOR ONE OR MORE MINUTES	INTERACTED WITH FOR FIVE OR MORE MINUTES	REQUESTED WHEN ITEM WAS NOT PRESENT OR OUT OF SIGHT
Hugs				
Massage				
Vibrating items				
Unusual textures				

Preference Assessment

AUDITORY STIMULI				
STIMULUS	PICKED FIRST FROM ARRAY OF 3-5 ITEMS	INTERACTED WITH FOR ONE OR MORE MINUTES	INTERACTED WITH FOR FIVE OR MORE MINUTES	REQUESTED WHEN ITEM WAS NOT PRESENT OR OUT OF SIGHT
Music				
Playing instruments				
Teacher or parent singing				

MOVEMENT STIMULI				
STIMULUS	PICKED FIRST FROM ARRAY OF 3-5 ITEMS	INTERACTED WITH FOR ONE OR MORE MINUTES	INTERACTED WITH FOR FIVE OR MORE MINUTES	REQUESTED WHEN ITEM WAS NOT PRESENT OR OUT OF SIGHT
Running				
Jumping				
Spinning				

Preference Assessment

OLFACTORY STIMULI

STIMULUS	PICKED FIRST FROM ARRAY OF 3–5 ITEMS	INTERACTED WITH FOR ONE OR MORE MINUTES	INTERACTED WITH FOR FIVE OR MORE MINUTES	REQUESTED WHEN ITEM WAS NOT PRESENT OR OUT OF SIGHT
Flowers				
Perfume				
Aroma from food				
Scratch & Sniff stickers				

GUSTATORY STIMULI

STIMULUS	PICKED FIRST FROM ARRAY OF 3–5 ITEMS	INTERACTED WITH FOR ONE OR MORE MINUTES	INTERACTED WITH FOR FIVE OR MORE MINUTES	REQUESTED WHEN ITEM WAS NOT PRESENT OR OUT OF SIGHT
Pizza				
Crackers				
Chewing				
Salty food or snacks				

Preference Assessment

SOCIAL STIMULI				
STIMULUS	PICKED FIRST FROM ARRAY OF 3-5 ITEMS	INTERACTED WITH FOR ONE OR MORE MINUTES	INTERACTED WITH FOR FIVE OR MORE MINUTES	REQUESTED WHEN ITEM WAS NOT PRESENT OR OUT OF SIGHT
Smiles				
High fives				
Singing together				
Interactive games				
Conversation				

VESTIBULAR STIMULI				
STIMULUS	PICKED FIRST FROM ARRAY OF 3-5 ITEMS	INTERACTED WITH FOR ONE OR MORE MINUTES	INTERACTED WITH FOR FIVE OR MORE MINUTES	REQUESTED WHEN ITEM WAS NOT PRESENT OR OUT OF SIGHT
Riding a bike				
Rocking				
Swinging				
Trampoline				

Preference Assessment

ELECTRONIC/COMPUTER STIMULI – List specific apps, computer games, and TV shows in the "Item" column				
ITEM	PICKED FIRST FROM ARRAY OF 3–5 ITEMS	INTERACTED WITH FOR ONE OR MORE MINUTES	INTERACTED WITH FOR FIVE OR MORE MINUTES	REQUESTED WHEN ITEM WAS NOT PRESENT OR OUT OF SIGHT

Preference Assessment

List items in order from most tally marks recorded to least tally marks recorded.

Parents report that the student is most interested in the items/activities below:

1. _____
2. _____
3. _____
4. _____
5. _____
6. _____
7. _____
8. _____
9. _____
10. _____
11. _____
12. _____
13. _____
14. _____
15. _____

1. _____
2. _____
3. _____
4. _____
5. _____

APPENDIX

B

Encouraging Social Interactions
and Conversations

Encouraging Social Interactions and Conversations

MANDING

Manding (or making requests) is the cornerstone of all future communication. When working with students who are struggling with communication, you may have "manding sessions" in which your primary goal is to practice having the student mand or request preferred items and activities. However, there are many opportunities to practice manding throughout the school day. Below are some suggestions for mands you can teach. It should be noted that the student should be motivated to receive the item or engage in the activity that you are teaching him/her to request. For example,

if your student does not like washing his/her hands, you should not teach that as a mand.

For students who struggle with acquiring and using language, you should utilize the free downloads available at www.avbpress.com/vb-mapp. The Intraverbal Subset and 240 Word List are especially helpful in setting individualized, developmentally appropriate goals for your students who are not yet ready for Kindergarten-level standards.

SNACK TIME/LUNCH
"Juice"
Sign for "Cookie"
"Pour" (water or milk)
"Wash hands"

COMPUTER ACTIVITIES
Name of specific program/app
"Type"
"Turn on computer"
"Push play"

CIRCLE TIME
Name of favorite song
Raising hand (request for attention)
"Can I be the helper?"
"Get up"

PLAYGROUND
Pulling you towards swings
"Push"
"Throw"
"Ball"

MATH MANIPULATIVES
"Stack" or "Build"
"Put together"
"Triangle" (or other shape)
"Six" (or other number card)

LINING UP
"Coat"
"Open door"
"Me first"
"Go"

READING
"Turn the page"
Name of book
"Read"
"Who's that?"

COMMUNITY WALK
"Go to store"
"Look!"
"My shoe's untied." (request for help)
Reaching hand towards yours

ART ACTIVITIES
Reaching for crayons
"I need a brush."
"Glue"
"Hang it up."

Encouraging Social Interactions and Conversations

EXAMPLES OF LEADING STATEMENTS

Below are samples for providing opportunities for students to ask "wh" questions. It is important to note that this is not a script, but shows potential responses the student could make. Your goal is to encourage natural conversation, so it is not considered incorrect if a student responds with a different type of question than you expected unless it doesn't make sense in context.

PROMPTING WHAT QUESTIONS	
TEACHER STATEMENT	**POTENTIAL STUDENT RESPONSE**
"You'll never believe what I saw this morning!"	"What did you see?"
"I had so much fun this weekend."	"What did you do?"
"I saw a terrible movie last night."	"What movie did you see?"
"Look at this bruise."	"What happened?"
"I played with a really silly toy today."	"What was the toy?"

PROMPTING WHO QUESTIONS	
TEACHER STATEMENT	**POTENTIAL STUDENT RESPONSE**
"Guess who I saw yesterday!"	"Who did you see?"
"Look at the gift I just got."	"Who gave it to you?"
"Do you know who wrote this book?"	"No. Who wrote it?"
"We're receiving a visit today."	"Who is visiting?"
"I drove here with two people."	"Who did you drive with?"

PROMPTING WHERE QUESTIONS	
TEACHER STATEMENT	**POTENTIAL STUDENT RESPONSE**
"I put your book in a special spot."	"Where did you put it?"
"Did you see the picture she drew?"	"No. Where is it?"
"I left my hat somewhere."	"Where did you leave it?"
"We're meeting them for dinner."	"Where are we meeting them?"
"I found the answer."	"Where did you find it?"

Encouraging Social Interactions and Conversations

PROMPTING WHEN QUESTIONS	
TEACHER STATEMENT	**POTENTIAL STUDENT RESPONSE**
"I saw that movie, too."	"When did you see it?"
"We are going to the store today."	"When are we going?"
"You wouldn't believe what time I woke up."	"When did you wake up?"
"I've had this shirt for a long time."	"When did you get it?"
"We can't look at the book yet."	"When can we look at it?"

PROMPTING WHY QUESTIONS	
TEACHER STATEMENT	**POTENTIAL STUDENT RESPONSE**
"I had to move the car."	"Why did you have to move the car?"
"We are having snack time earlier today."	"Why is snack time earlier?"
"My foot is still hurting."	"Why is it hurting?"
"We can't use the computer today."	"Why not?"
"The playground is closed."	"Why is it closed?"

APPENDIX

C

Differentiated Instruction Cubes Template
Directions and Suggestions

Differentiated Instruction Cubes Template
Directions and Suggestions

This page can be reproduced to create customized activities for use with the *Differentiated Instruction Cubes*. Just photocopy the templates below and add the pertinent information or activity, cut, and then place into the sides of the cubes. You'll also find word lists, activities, questions and suggestions for specific standards listed by their CCSS code.

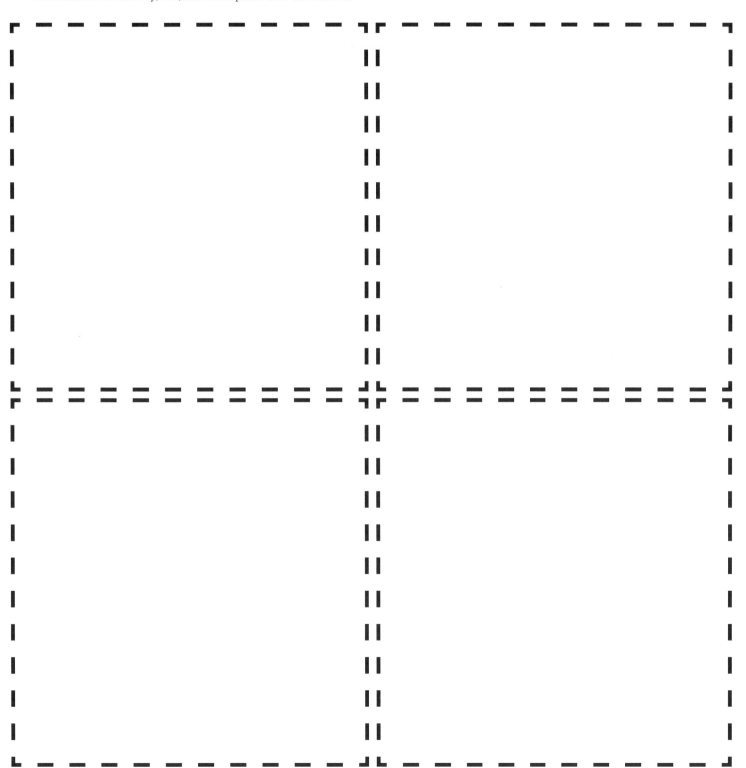

Differentiated Instruction Cubes Template Directions and Suggestions

RL.K.6, RI.K.6

Students take turns rolling the cube and responding to the question.

- Who is the author?
- Who is the illustrator?
- Who wrote the book?
- Who illustrated the book?
- What does an author do?
- What does an illustrator do?

RI.K.5

Students take turns rolling the cubes, then responding to the prompt.

- Point to the cover of the book.
- Where is the spine of the book?
- Touch the front cover.
- Where is the title page?
- Show me the back cover.
- Touch a page in the book.
- What can you find on the front cover?
- What can you find on the back cover?
- What can you find on the spine?
- Where do you find the title?
- Show me who wrote the book.
- What can you find on the title page?

RL.K.7, RI.K.7

Students take turns rolling the cube and responding to the question.

- What part of the story does the illustration show?
- What is happening in this illustration?
- Who is shown in this illustration?
- What happened in the story?
- Describe the illustration. What does it show about the story?
- What is the setting in this illustration?

RI.K.9

Students take turns rolling the cube and responding to the prompt.

- Name one similarity between the two texts.
- Name one difference between the two texts.
- Name one similarity between the illustrations of the two texts.
- Name one difference between the illustrations of the two texts.
- Tell a peer about one fact you learned.
- Show a peer a picture from each text and compare them in one sentence.

Differentiated Instruction Cubes Template Directions and Suggestions

W.K.5

After one student's work is shared, have each student roll the cube and respond.

- One thing I liked is _____ .
- I think _____ would be better if _____ .
- The story made me feel _____ .
- I didn't understand _____ .
- My favorite part is _____ .
- I want to know more about _____ .

W.K.7

After this activity, the student should pick one of these questions to write or draw about.

- What is your favorite book by this author?
- Pick one story. What is one thing you did not like about this story?
- Tell me about an illustration from this author's books.
- Does this author write about one character or many characters?
- What type of stories does this author write?
- Pick one story. What did the main character learn?

L.K.2.b

Students take turns rolling the cube and either responding to the prompt or naming the punctuation mark.

.

?

!

Draw a period.

Draw a question mark.

Draw an exclamation mark.

L.K.4.a

Use each word in two sentences, illustrating the word's two meanings.

duck	fair	ring
fly	foot	pet
close	hard	stick
bat	left	tire
bark	nail	seal
dress	park	star

Differentiated Instruction Cubes Template Directions and Suggestions

L.K.5.b

After the student rolls one of these words, he/she must identify its antonym.

Verbs	Adjectives
walk	slow
run	fast
whisper	loud
shout	quiet
stop	big
go	small
sleep	old
wake up	new
push	easy
pull	hard
float	full
sink	empty
throw	hot
catch	cold
sit	heavy
stand	light
laugh	short
cry	long

L.K.5.c

Play this as an "I Spy" game. When the student rolls a word, he/she has to use a complete sentence to describe a space in the environment that fits the description. For students who have mastered this, they can describe a space in any environment that fits the description.

colorful	dangerous	short
empty	loud	long
wide	quiet	old
clean	friendly	new
beautiful	small	soft
safe	tall	hard

L.K.5.d

This should be played as an active game. One student rolls a die, and all students must do as instructed. It's helpful to have an auditory signal to end each round, such as a bell or timer.

walk	talk	jump
prance	whisper	skip
march	shout	hop
clap	touch	draw
knock	pet	write
pat	rub	scribble

Differentiated Instruction Cubes Template Directions and Suggestions

K.CC.A.2

Choose the appropriate level for your student. The student rolls the die, then must "count on" from that number. If your student has mastered all three levels, you can challenge him/her to count backwards from the number rolled.

Level One	Level Two	Level Three
1	5	11
2	6	12
3	7	13
2	8	14
3	9	15
4	10	16

K.CC.C.7

There are two ways to play this game. One is to have the student roll two dice, then compare the numbers by writing the correct symbol on a piece of paper or dry erase board and correctly placing the dice. The other is to have the student roll three dice (two with numbers and one with a symbol) and have him/her arrange the dice to form a correct number sentence. For the second game, if the student rolls an equal sign, he/she can re-roll one die until he/she is able to create a correct number sentence.

Dice One	Dice Two	Dice Three
1	2	<
3	4	<
5	6	>
7	8	>
9	10	>
8	3	=

APPENDIX

D

Data Sheets and Samples

Per Opportunity Individual Data Sheet

Teaching Procedure: The following should be explained in detail for each step: date implemented, pre-test score, number of trials per session, S[D], response definition, prompt level, error correction procedure, and mastery criterion.

Computation Procedure: Take the total number of correct responses and divide by the total number of opportunities and multiply by 100 for a percentage (# correct ÷ # of opportunities x 100 = %). Graph accordingly on the corresponding *Per Opportunity Graph*.

Per Opportunity Individual Data Sheet

STUDENT: *Stephanie*   STRAND/DOMAIN: *Geometry*

PROMPT LEVEL ABBREVIATIONS:

FPP — Full Physical Prompt   M — Modeling   VP — Verbal Prompt
PPP — Partial Physical Prompt   GP — Gestural Prompt   VSP — Visual Prompt

DATE	CCSS CODE	TARGET	PROMPT LEVELS AND RESPONSE RECORDING (Y/N)										PERCENT CORRECT	INSTRUCTOR INITIALS
2/11/14	KGA2	Triangle	Ⓨ N	Ⓨ N	Ⓨ N	Ⓨ N	Y Ⓝ	Ⓨ N	Y Ⓝ	Ⓨ N			70%	TR
					GP		GP		GP					
2/12/14	KGA2	Triangle	Y Ⓝ	Ⓨ N	Ⓨ N	Ⓨ N	Ⓨ N	Ⓨ N	Ⓨ N	Y Ⓝ			80%	TR
			GP	GP										
			Y/N	Y/N	Y/N	Y/N	Y/N	Y/N	Y/N	Y/N	Y/N	Y/N		
			Y/N	Y/N	Y/N	Y/N	Y/N	Y/N	Y/N	Y/N	Y/N	Y/N		
			Y/N	Y/N	Y/N	Y/N	Y/N	Y/N	Y/N	Y/N	Y/N	Y/N		
			Y/N	Y/N	Y/N	Y/N	Y/N	Y/N	Y/N	Y/N	Y/N	Y/N		
			Y/N	Y/N	Y/N	Y/N	Y/N	Y/N	Y/N	Y/N	Y/N	Y/N		
			Y/N	Y/N	Y/N	Y/N	Y/N	Y/N	Y/N	Y/N	Y/N	Y/N		
			Y/N	Y/N	Y/N	Y/N	Y/N	Y/N	Y/N	Y/N	Y/N	Y/N		

Per Opportunity Individual Data Sheet

STUDENT: _____

STRAND/DOMAIN: _____

PROMPT LEVEL ABBREVIATIONS:

FPP — Full Physical Prompt
PPP — Partial Physical Prompt

M — Modeling
GP — Gestural Prompt

VP — Verbal Prompt
VSP — Visual Prompt

DATE	CCSS CODE	TARGET	PROMPT LEVELS AND RESPONSE RECORDING (Y/N)							PERCENT CORRECT	INSTRUCTOR INITIALS
			Y/N	Y/N	Y/N	Y/N	Y/N	Y/N	Y/N		
			Y/N	Y/N	Y/N	Y/N	Y/N	Y/N	Y/N		
			Y/N	Y/N	Y/N	Y/N	Y/N	Y/N	Y/N		
			Y/N	Y/N	Y/N	Y/N	Y/N	Y/N	Y/N		
			Y/N	Y/N	Y/N	Y/N	Y/N	Y/N	Y/N		
			Y/N	Y/N	Y/N	Y/N	Y/N	Y/N	Y/N		
			Y/N	Y/N	Y/N	Y/N	Y/N	Y/N	Y/N		
			Y/N	Y/N	Y/N	Y/N	Y/N	Y/N	Y/N		
			Y/N	Y/N	Y/N	Y/N	Y/N	Y/N	Y/N		

Per Opportunity Group Data Sheet

For this example, the teacher was doing a whole group geometry lesson on the *All Around Learning Circle Time Activity Set* mat. She had this data sheet on a clipboard so she could take data for all of the students during the activity. (It may also be beneficial to have a paraprofessional take data while you conduct the activity.) She mixed in mastered questions with the questions focused on the target skill, but only marked Yes or No for the questions focused on the target skill. She only circled Y for a student if the student independently responded correctly without any prompts. She was able to use the mat as well as shape cards to practice the target skills, rotating around the group and providing appropriate reinforcement for correct responses as well as for appropriate circle time behaviors.

Per Opportunity Group Data Sheet

PROGRAM: *Geometry*   CCSS: *KGA2 / KGB4*

STUDENT	TARGET	RESPONSES										PERCENT CORRECT
Carlos	circle	Ⓨ/N	Ⓨ/N	Y/Ⓝ	Ⓨ/N	Ⓨ/N	Ⓨ/N	Ⓨ/N	y/Ⓝ	Ⓨ/N	Ⓨ/N	60%
Mark	heart	y/Ⓝ	Ⓨ/N	Ⓨ/N	Ⓨ/N	y/Ⓝ	y/Ⓝ	Ⓨ/N	y/Ⓝ	Y/Ⓝ	Ⓨ/N	40%
Lisa	diamond	Ⓨ/N	Ⓨ/N	Ⓨ/N	Ⓨ/N	Ⓨ/N	Ⓨ/N	Ⓨ/N	Ⓨ/N	Ⓨ/N	Ⓨ/N	100%
James	comparing # of sides of two shapes	Ⓨ/N	Y/Ⓝ	Ⓨ/N	Ⓨ/N	Ⓨ/N	Y/Ⓝ	Y/Ⓝ	Ⓨ/N	Y/Ⓝ	Y/Ⓝ	50%
Diego	diamond	Y/Ⓝ	y/Ⓝ	Ⓨ/N	y/Ⓝ	Ⓨ/N	Y/Ⓝ	Ⓨ/N	Ⓨ/N	Ⓨ/N	y/Ⓝ	30%
Daquan	star	Ⓨ/N	Ⓨ/N	Ⓨ/N	Ⓨ/N	Ⓨ/N	Ⓨ/N	Y/Ⓝ	Ⓨ/N	Ⓨ/N	Y/Ⓝ	80%

Per Opportunity Group Data Sheet

PROGRAM: _____

CCSS: _____

STUDENT	TARGET	RESPONSES					PERCENT CORRECT
		Y / N	Y / N	Y / N	Y / N	Y / N	
		Y / N	Y / N	Y / N	Y / N	Y / N	
		Y / N	Y / N	Y / N	Y / N	Y / N	
		Y / N	Y / N	Y / N	Y / N	Y / N	
		Y / N	Y / N	Y / N	Y / N	Y / N	
		Y / N	Y / N	Y / N	Y / N	Y / N	
		Y / N	Y / N	Y / N	Y / N	Y / N	
		Y / N	Y / N	Y / N	Y / N	Y / N	
		Y / N	Y / N	Y / N	Y / N	Y / N	
		Y / N	Y / N	Y / N	Y / N	Y / N	
		Y / N	Y / N	Y / N	Y / N	Y / N	
		Y / N	Y / N	Y / N	Y / N	Y / N	

Per Opportunity Graph

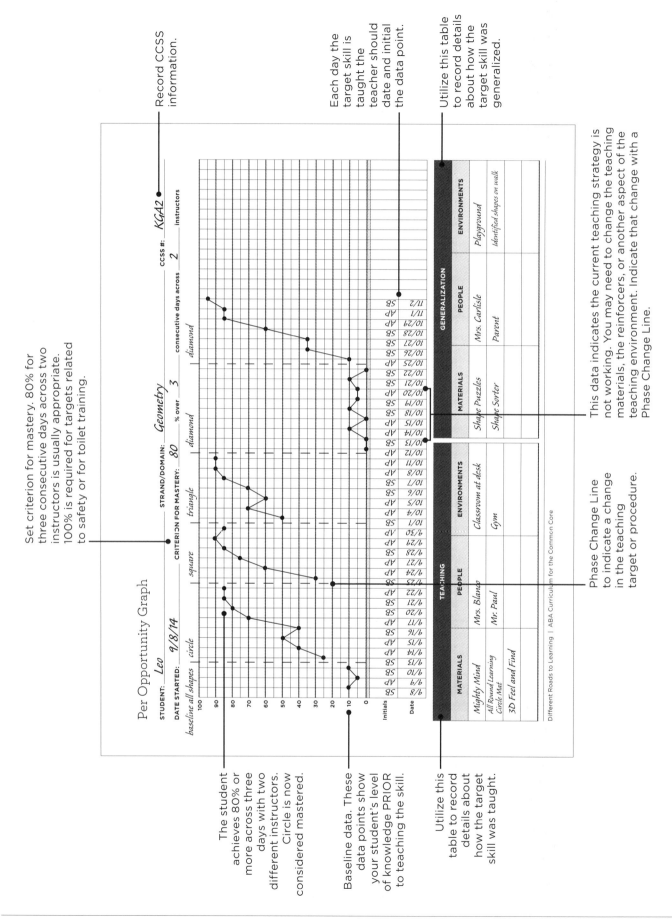

Record CCSS information.

Each day the target skill is taught the teacher should date and initial the data point.

Utilize this table to record details about how the target skill was generalized.

Set criterion for mastery. 80% for three consecutive days across two instructors is usually appropriate. 100% is required for targets related to safety or for toilet training.

Per Opportunity Graph

STUDENT: Leo   STRAND/DOMAIN: Geometry   CCSS #: KGA2

DATE STARTED: 9/8/14   CRITERION FOR MASTERY: 80   % over 3   consecutive days across 2 instructors

The student achieves 80% or more across three days with two different instructors. Circle is now considered mastered.

Baseline data. These data points show your student's level of knowledge PRIOR to teaching the skill.

Utilize this table to record details about how the target skill was taught.

This data indicates the current teaching strategy is not working. You may need to change the teaching materials, the reinforcers, or another aspect of the teaching environment. Indicate that change with a Phase Change Line.

Phase Change Line to indicate a change in the teaching target or procedure.

TEACHING		
MATERIALS	PEOPLE	ENVIRONMENTS
Mighty Mind	Mrs. Blanco	Classroom at desk
All Round Learning Circle Mat	Mr. Paul	Gym
3D Feel and Find		

GENERALIZATION		
MATERIALS	PEOPLE	ENVIRONMENTS
Shape Puzzles	Mrs. Carlisle	Playground
Shape Sorter	Parent	Identified shapes on walk

Different Roads to Learning | ABA Curriculum for the Common Core

Per Opportunity Graph

STUDENT: _____ STRAND/DOMAIN: _____ CCSS #: _____

DATE STARTED: _____ CRITERION FOR MASTERY: _____ % over _____ consecutive days across _____ instructors

100																								
90																								
80																								
70																								
60																								
50																								
40																								
30																								
20																								
10																								
0																								
Initials																								
Date																								

TEACHING

MATERIALS	PEOPLE	ENVIRONMENTS

GENERALIZATION

MATERIALS	PEOPLE	ENVIRONMENTS

Task Analysis: *Total Task*

Below is a sample of a task analysis created for the skill of washing hands. The student earns a + for independently completing the step. If any type of prompt is required, the prompt level is recorded next to the step. At the bottom, the percentage correct is determined by dividing the number of independently performed steps by the total number of steps.

A task analysis can be completed in one of three ways. The first is a whole task analysis, in which the student is taught the entire chain of tasks at the same time.

The second is forward chaining, in which the student is taught the first step in the chain, while all other steps are done for them. Once that step is mastered, the student is then taught the next step and expected to do the first and second step independently. This continues until all steps are learned.

The final way to teach a task analysis is through backwards chaining. This is similar to forward chaining, except the adult does all the steps for the child, and the child completes the last step. Once the student has mastered that step, then they are taught the next-to-last step and expected to do that and the last step independently. This continues until all steps are learned.

Task Analysis: *Total Task*

STUDENT: *Brian*   TASK: *Washing hands*   DATE PROGRAM STARTED: *02/01/14*

PROMPT LEVEL ABBREVIATIONS:

FPP — Full Physical Prompt   M — Modeling   VP — Verbal Prompt
PPP — Partial Physical Prompt GP — Gestural Prompt   VSP — Visual Prompt

DATE	02/01	02/02	02/03	02/04	02/05	02/08	02/09	02/10					
STEP # / COMPONENT SKILL				PROMPT LEVELS									
1 Push up sleeves (if necessary)	FPP	PPP	PPP	GP	+	+	+	+					
2 Turn on water	FPP	FPP	PPP	PPP	PPP	VP	VP	VP					
3 Wet hands	PPP	+	+	+	+	+	+	+					
4 Push pump to put soap in hand	FPP	FPP	PPP	PPP	+	+	+	+					
5 Scrub hands for 10 seconds	FPP	PPP	PPP	GP	GP	+	+	+					
6 Rinse hands	FPP	GP	+	+	+	+	+	+					
7 Turn off water	FPP	GP	+	+	+	+	+	+					
8 Dry hands on towel	FPP	FPP	PPP	PPP	PPP	GP	GP	GP					
PERCENT CORRECT	0%	12.5%	37.5%	37.5%	62.5%	75%	75%	75%					

Different Roads to Learning | ABA Curriculum for the Common Core

Task Analysis: *Forward Chaining*

For this example, the teacher starts by teaching the student to independently push up his sleeves. Once he has done that independently two times in a row, the teacher introduces the next step.

Task Analysis: *Forward Chaining*

STUDENT: *Brian*   TASK: *Washing hands*   DATE PROGRAM STARTED: *02/01/14*

PROMPT LEVEL ABBREVIATIONS:

FPP — Full Physical Prompt
PPP — Partial Physical Prompt
M — Modeling
GP — Gestural Prompt
VP — Verbal Prompt
VSP — Visual Prompt

STEP #	COMPONENT SKILL	DATE							
		02/01	02/02	02/03	02/04	02/05	02/08	02/09	02/10
		PROMPT LEVELS							
1	Push up sleeves (if necessary)	PPP	PPP	GP	+	+	+	+	+
2	Turn on water					GP	GP	+	+
3	Wet hands								GP
4	Push pump to put soap in hand								
5	Scrub hands for 10 seconds								
6	Rinse hands								
7	Turn off water								
8	Dry hands on towel								
PERCENT CORRECT		0%	0%	0%	12.5%	12.5%	12.5%	25%	25%

Different Roads to Learning | ABA Curriculum for the Common Core

For this example, the teacher starts by teaching the student to independently dry his hands after the teacher has taken him through all the other steps. Once he has done that independently two times in a row, the teacher introduces the previous step.

Task Analysis: *Backward Chaining*

STUDENT: *Brian*   TASK: *Washing hands*   DATE PROGRAM STARTED: *02/01/14*

PROMPT LEVEL ABBREVIATIONS:

FPP — Full Physical Prompt   M — Modeling   VP — Verbal Prompt
PPP — Partial Physical Prompt   GP — Gestural Prompt   VSP — Visual Prompt

STEP #	DATE / COMPONENT SKILL	02/01	02/02	02/03	02/04	02/05	02/08	02/09	02/10
					PROMPT LEVELS				
1	Push up sleeves (if necessary)								
2	Turn on water								
3	Wet hands								
4	Push pump to put soap in hand								
5	Scrub hands for 10 seconds								
6	Rinse hands						PPP	PPP	PPP
7	Turn off water				GP	+	+	+	+
8	Dry hands on towel	PPP	GP	+	+	+	+	+	+
	PERCENT CORRECT	0%	0%	12.5%	12.5%	25%	25%	25%	25%

Task Analysis: _____

STUDENT: _____

TASK: _____

DATE PROGRAM STARTED: _____

PROMPT LEVEL ABBREVIATIONS:

FPP — Full Physical Prompt

PPP — Partial Physical Prompt

M — Modeling

GP — Gestural Prompt

VP — Verbal Prompt

VSP — Visual Prompt

STEP #	COMPONENT SKILL	DATE	PROMPT LEVELS									
	PERCENT CORRECT											

References

Application to students with disabilities. (2014).
Retrieved from http://corestandards.org/assets/application-to-students-with-disabilities.pdf

Cooper, J.O., Heron, T.E., & Heward, W.L. (2007). Applied behavior analysis (2nd ed.).
Upper Saddle River, NJ: Pearson Prentice Hall.

Fovel, J.T. (2013). The new ABA program companion. M.F. Danielski (Ed.). New York, NY: DRL Books.

Larsson, E.V., & Wright, S. (2011). I. Ovar Lovaas (1927–2010). *The Behavior Analyst, 34*(1): 111–114.

Leaf, R., & McEachin, J. (Eds.). (1999). A work in progress. New York, NY: DRL Books.

Lovaas, O.I. (1987). Behavioral treatment and normal educational and intellectual functioning
in young autistic children. Journal of Consulting and Clinical Psychology, 55, 3-9.

McClannahan, L.E., & Kranz, P.J. (2005). Teaching conversation to children with autism:
Scripts and script fading. Bethesda, MD: Woodbine House.

McEachin, J.J., Smith, T., & Lovaas, O.I. (1993). Long-term outcome for children with autism who received
early intensive behavioral treatment. American Journal on Mental Retardation, 97(4): 359-372.

Rispoli, M., O'Reilly, M., Lang, R., Machalicek, W., Davis, T., Lancioni, Giulio, & Sigafoos, J. (2011).
Effects of Motivating Operations on Problem and Academic Behavior in Classrooms.
Journal of Applied Behavior Analysis, 44, 187-192.

Sundberg, M.L., & Partington, J.W. (1999). The need for both discrete trial and natural environment
language training for children with autism. In P.M. Ghezzi, W.L. Williams, & J.E. Carr (Eds.),
Autism: Behavior-analytic perspectives (pp. 139-156). Reno, NJ: Context Press.

Taylor, B.A., & Harris, S.L. (1995). Teaching children with autism to seek information:
Acquisition of novel information and generalization of responding.
Journal of Applied Behavior Analysis, 28, 3-14.

Weiss, M.J., & Valbona, D. (2011). Jumpstarting communication skills in children with autism.
Bethesda, MD: Woodbine House.